WITHDRAWN

VOICE THERAPY AND VOICE IMPROVEMENT

VOICE THERAPY
and
VOICE IMPROVEMENT

*A Simple and Practical Approach
Through Correct Muscle Usage*

By

WALTER SCHUMACHER

*Affiliate Member
The Royal Society of Medicine, London
Member
The American Speech and Hearing Association
The California Speech and Hearing Association*

CHARLES C THOMAS • PUBLISHER
Springfield • Illinois • U.S.A.

Published and Distributed Throughout the World by

CHARLES C THOMAS • PUBLISHER

Bannerstone House

301-327 East Lawrence Avenue, Springfield, Illinois, U.S.A.

© *1974, by* CHARLES C THOMAS • PUBLISHER

ISBN 0–398–0–398–02920–2

Library of Congress Catalog Card Number: 73–7918

*With THOMAS BOOKS careful attention is given to all details of
manufacturing and design. It is the Publisher's desire to present books that are
satisfactory as to their physical qualities and artistic possibilities and
appropriate for their particular use. THOMAS BOOKS will be true to those
laws of quality that assure a good name and good will.*

Library of Congress Cataloging in Publication Data
Schumacher, Walter, 1903–
  Voice therapy and voice improvement.
  1. Voice culture. I. Title.
DNLM: 1. Speech therapy. 2. Voice. 3. Voice
training. WV500 S392v 1973
PN4162.S362   784.9'32   73–7918
  ISBn 0–398–02920–2

Printed in the United States of America

BB–14

To MIRIAM M. ELKUS,
who pioneered this approach to
voice therapy and voice improvement.

PREFACE

I BECAME PARTICULARLY interested in voices during my college days when I was accompanying singers at recitals and at vocal studios. During this time I listened with great interest to discussions among vocal students and teachers. Their topics ranged from methods to ideas and theories regarding voice production, many of which appeared to me to be very confusing and conflicting.

When visiting in San Francisco shortly after finishing college, I met Miriam M. Elkus, who was then helping speakers and singers with their vocal difficulties. I went to her studio accompanied by a singer who was having some difficulty with his voice. As she discussed his vocal problems with him, I realized that, for the first time, I was listening to someone whose work was not based on academic theories. She was showing him in a simple, practical and easily understandable manner how the way in which he was using the muscles of his vocal instrument was causing his problems and suggested what he should do about them in order to overcome his difficulties.

Mrs. Elkus told us she had sung for many years but that she had lost her speaking and singing voice by using the muscles of her vocal instrument improperly over a number of years. Later, her voice was restored through study and practice based on the findings of Dr. H. Holbrook Curtis who wrote of his research and work with singers in his book, *Voice Building and Tone Placing*. In the preface to his book, Dr. Curtis states that "the tangled skein of theories which one must unravel in order to arrive at any simple conclusion in regard to the singing voice, makes our endeavor in the present volume an arduous one"

After her own voice was restored, Mrs. Elkus began helping

other speakers and singers who were having vocal difficulties. She continued to enlarge upon the work begun by Dr. Curtis, working in cooperation with prominent laryngologists in San Francisco, particularly Dr. Grant L. Selfridge, Dr. Lewis F. Morrison and Dr. Robert C. Martin.

When I returned to San Francisco several years later, I became associated with Mrs. Elkus in her work. Since her retirement I have carried on this approach to voice therapy and voice improvement through correct muscle usage and further developed it to where it is now recognized both nationally and internationally.

I hope that this book will help to further untangle the skein of theories that still exist regarding the production of sound, both for speaking and for singing, and that it will be of help to those persons seeking information regarding their own vocal problems.

683 Sutter Street   WALTER SCHUMACHER
San Francisco, California 94102

ACKNOWLEDGMENTS

I wish to acknowledge and thank the following persons for their assistance in the preparation of this book:

Richard J. Elkus for his suggestions, comments and guidance.

Michael Moreskine for the photography.

John Owen Douglass for his assistance with the original photographs.

Bernie D. Larr for his editorial assistance.

CONTENTS

VOICE THERAPY AND VOICE IMPROVEMENT

Chapter One

A SIMPLE AND

PRACTICAL APPROACH

THIS BOOK PRESENTS in simple form, a practical approach to voice therapy and voice improvement.

It makes clear in simple language the correct usage of the muscles of the vocal instrument when speaking and singing. Although the vocal instrument involves the entire body, in this approach to voice therapy and voice improvement we are principally concerned with the muscles of the cheeks, nose, lips, lower jaw, tongue, soft palate and waist.

This approach places the emphasis on the correct usage of the muscles which produce the voice and not on the voice itself. It recognizes that the voice is the effect, that the muscles are the cause. When the muscles are used correctly, the voice will be correct.

In this book you are shown how to exercise the muscles of your vocal instrument correctly in order to keep them in good physical condition and how to use them correctly when you speak and sing.

Through the continued correct usage of these muscles, your voice becomes of the best quality that your own particular vocal instrument is capable of producing.

VOICE THERAPY

If you are suffering from any physical discomfort when speaking or singing such as hoarseness, strain or fatigue and your physician indicates that it is due to your manner of speaking or singing, you can use these exercises to help yourself out of your difficulty. However, *you must have your physician's approval* before using the exercises and then you must

3

check with him regularly as to the results of the work you are doing.

If you are a voice therapist, these exercises may be used in cooperation with the laryngologist in the treatment of voice disorders.

This approach to voice therapy is a physiotherapy. The voice therapist works in cooperation with the laryngologist in showing his patients how to exercise and use the muscles of their vocal instruments correctly just as any other physiotherapist works in cooperation with the physician or surgeon in showing his patients how to exercise and use other muscles of their bodies correctly.

As indicated, the muscles of the vocal instrument with which we are particularly concerned in this type of voice therapy are those of the cheeks, nose, lips, lower jaw, tongue, soft palate and waist.

When any of these muscles are used incorrectly in speaking or singing, a strain is placed on the muscles of the larynx and vocal cords. This strain can result in the hoarseness, discomfort and fatigue which the patient feels and the vocal nodules, contact ulcers, thickening of the vocal cords and other ailments of the larynx and vocal cords which the physician sees.

When the patient is taught and understands how to keep these muscles in good physical condition and how to use them properly when he speaks or sings, the muscles of the larynx and vocal cords are free to function normally. Through this correct functioning the voice also becomes free and of a normal quality.

When damage has been done to one or both vocal cords, the muscles are restored as near to normal as the damage to the muscles will permit. Thus the voice is also restored as near to normal as the damage to the muscles will permit.

VOICE IMPROVEMENT

Since the exercises used in voice therapy are fundamental to the correct production of sound when speaking and singing, these same exercises are also used to show the speaker and singer how to improve his speaking and singing voice.

Using these exercises can improve your speaking voice for use in your daily conversation, in your business or profession, for public speaking and for acting in the theatre. They have been used extensively by attorneys, teachers, clergymen, salesmen, engineers, architects, telephone operators, receptionists, supervisors of personnel and others.

They can also be used to assist in overcoming speech difficulties such as poor articulation, lisping and stuttering and in eliminating foreign or local accents. In fact, they are of value in any type of speech difficulty where the muscles involved in speaking are capable of being exercised and used.

Particular success has been achieved in the area of singing, whether it be popular songs, show tunes, musical comedy, light opera or opera.

The exercises have been used extensively with singers whose voices have been impaired or lost through methods of voice production that have been detrimental to the muscles of the vocal instrument.

If you are a parent and are interested in your child's voice, the use of these exercises will help to prevent voice disorders or speech difficulties from occuring later in life.

These exercises can be used to improve the voice quality of the deaf and hard of hearing child and adult, in cooperation with the orthodontist and oral surgeon in correcting misusage of the oral and facial muscles and in cooperation with the plastic surgeon in correctly strengthening the facial muscles.

Chapter Two

HOW TO USE THE BOOK

THE CHAPTERS THAT follow are arranged as a series of lessons as I give them to students at my studio.

In the studio I cover the exercises in a course of six lessons. However, since you have to be your own teacher with the assistance of this book, I have arranged them in a slightly longer series, covering less work in each lesson or chapter.

In these chapters you are shown how to exercise the muscles of your vocal instrument in order to keep them in good physical condition and how to use them correctly when you speak and sing.

It is like going to a gymnasium for exercises for other muscles of your body, but these are for the muscles you use when you speak and sing.

You have to do the work yourself and in the order given. It is absolutely necessary that you read, understand and practice the exercises in this order in order to get the results you want, the kind of voice you want.

All of the exercises are very simple and easy to understand and do. However, unless you can do them correctly, you cannot use your muscles properly when you speak or sing.

You should have fun with the exercises. Do not make a job of them. Having fun with them releases tense and constricted muscles and permits you to begin using them correctly.

Do them when you get up in the morning, before you go to bed at night and at any other time of the day when you think of it. You do not have to have any set time for practice. Many students do them when driving to and from work.

You should do the exercises given in each chapter for approximately one week before going on to the next. This gives you plenty of time to read, understand and do the exercises given before going on to new ones.

Since I cannot demonstrate the exercises for you myself as I do for students in my studio, you will have to study the pictures and read the instructions carefully. Then use your mirror to see that you are doing them correctly. Your mirror is your best friend.

The pictures shown are not intended as exact muscle positions for you to imitate. Each person's vocal instrument is individual and may be constructed by nature in a slightly different manner from that of another person. However, the basic principles of correct muscle usage when speaking and singing are the same. The pictures are to be taken as examples of correct muscle usage to help you in exercising and using your own muscles correctly but not as exact muscle positions for you to copy.

If you are a singer or are particularly interested in singing, you can begin the singing exercises sooner by combining them with the chapters with the muscle and speech exercises as follows:

Chapter 13 with chapter 4
Chapter 14 with chapter 6
Chapter 15 with chapter 8
Chapter 16 with chapter 9
Chapter 17 with chapter 10

I give the singing exercises along with the muscle and speech exercises in this way at my studio. However, I felt it would be easier for the student who is not a singer and is teaching himself with this book to do the muscle and speech exercises first and then continue with the singing exercises.

Chapter Three

BEFORE YOU BEGIN
YOUR FIRST LESSON

BEFORE WE BEGIN the first lesson at my studio, we make a tape recording of the student's voice. At the end of the lesson we make another recording. Then we play them both back. In this way the student can hear for himself the improvement that can result from following the instructions given in his first lesson. We keep these recordings permanently so that he can compare them with later recordings. In this way he can hear how his voice improves in quality, resonance and volume as he learns how to exercise and use the muscles of his vocal instrument correctly.

If you have a tape recorder or have a friend who will make a recording for you, make a recording of your voice before you begin the next chapter, which is your first lesson. I usually use a portion of the *Gettysburg Address* as everyone is familiar with it and it is simple and easy to read. Read it just as if you were talking to someone so that you can hear your own natural speaking voice. Keep the recording so that you can compare it with the one you will make after you have gone over the work in your first lesson.

Four score and seven years ago our fathers brought forth upon this continent a new nation, conceived in liberty and dedicated to the proposition that all men are created equal.

Now we are engaged in a great civil war, testing whether that nation, or any nation so conceived and so dedicated, can long endure.

We are met on a great battle field of that war. We have come to dedicate a portion of that field as a final resting place for those who here gave their lives that that nation might live. It is altogether fitting and proper that we should do this.

If you would like to see how your facial expression changes as you learn to use your facial muscles correctly, have pictures taken of yourself saying "See" and "Sah" before you begin the next chapter. I use a small camera which takes pictures of the face at a distance of two feet. Then have another set taken saying the same sounds of "See" and "Sah" when you have completed your lessons.

You can then see for yourself how your facial expression has changed, how alive and interesting it has become. The correct usage of the muscles that keeps your voice alive and interesting also helps to keep the expression on your face alive and interesting.

Figure 1A.
Incorrect Usage

Figure 1B.
Exaggerated Usage
For Practice

Figure 1C.
Normal Usage

Usage of the Upper Facial Muscles
When Speaking and Singing

Chapter Four

THE CHEEKS

THE FIRST SET OF muscles of the vocal instrument we become acquainted with are those of the cheeks.

They are a very important set of muscles of the vocal instrument. If they are not used correctly when speaking and singing, other muscles such as those of the lips, tongue and soft palate cannot be used correctly. That is why we learn how to use them correctly first. It is of no use to work on the muscles of the lips, tongue or soft palate unless the muscles of the cheeks are used correctly.

These muscles of the cheeks cover part of the bone structure and cavities of the head which are the most important resonators of the vocal instrument.

They must be correctly strengthened so that they can remain lifted at all times when speaking and singing, as in the picture on the right on the opposite page. The upper teeth must always be in view. This lift of the cheeks allows the vibrating air or breath to float up to the resonating bone structure and cavities of the head and brings life and resonance to the voice. When they are sagging or collapsed, as in the picture on the left, they act as a muffler to the voice. The vibrating air cannot float up to the resonators as it should and the voice becomes dead, dull and uninteresting.

All of the cases of ailments of the larynx referred to me over the years have had these collapsed facial muscles. In many cases the muscles have not been used for so long that it is impossible for the patient or student to move them at all at first.

We use the following exercise for correctly strengthening the muscles of the cheeks and keeping them in good physical condition.

11

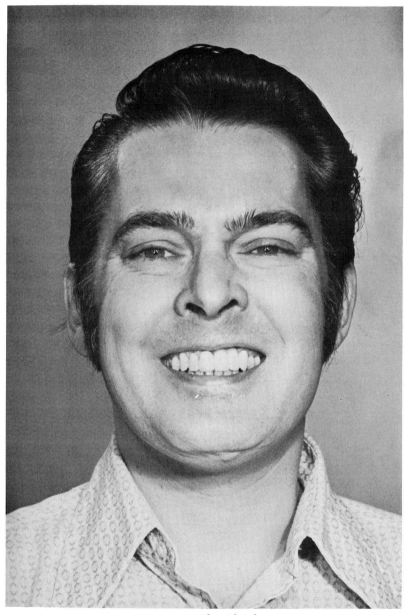

Figure 2. The Cheeks

Take a mirror and look at your face.

Try to lift the muscles of your cheeks high up under your eyes as shown in Figure 2.

Be sure to keep your lips apart so that your upper teeth come into view with each lift.

Hold them up for a moment.

Let them drop.

Lift them again.

Let them drop.

Lift them.

Let them drop.

Some students have no difficulty in lifting the muscles of their cheeks. However, it is necessary to do the exercise occasionally in order to keep them strong and in good physical condition.

If you do find it a bit difficult to move the muscles at first, keep on trying and they will soon begin to move up and down for you. I have had students who could not move them at all at first.

Don't do the exercise too rapidly. Hold the muscles up for a short time each time you lift them so that they get the full benefit of the exercise. Continue to practice lifting and dropping them whenever you think of it, whenever no one is watching you. Have fun with the exercise. After doing it for a while, you will find that your cheeks will move up and down quite easily.

You should keep on doing this exercise as long as you continue to speak or sing. As we grow older the facial muscles have a tendency to drop. This drop or collapse gives the face the appearance of age. By keeping them thoroughly strengthened and lifted you keep the appearance of youth and life in your face.

After you have exercised your cheeks for a while and it becomes easy for you to lift them, try the following two exercises for using them when you are making sounds.

SEE ME PLEASE

Try saying the words "See Me Please" with your cheeks lifted high up under your eyes as in the picture for the cheek muscle exercise.

Say each word as if you were asking a question, like this:
See? Me? Please?

Saying the words as if you were asking questions helps to bring your voice to its own proper muscle level. Most of us speak on too low a muscle level. By low muscle level I mean speaking down on the muscles of the throat. When we do this the sounds we make cannot float properly up to the resonating structure of the upper part of the head. When you are speaking on your own correct muscle level, the feeling is that your voice is floating from your ears up.

If you feel that your voice is too high or too light, saying the words as if you were asking questions and feeling as if the sounds you are making were floating freely and easily from your ears up can also help to bring your voice to its proper muscle level.

I have had people referred to me by their physicians because of thickening of the vocal cords and vocal nodules who had thought their voices were too high or too light and had tried to make them lower or bigger by trying to lower their voices. Trying to lower their voices without knowing what they were doing muscularly had caused them to speak on too low a muscle level and had resulted in the thickening of the vocal cords and vocal nodules.

Be sure to lift your cheeks each time before you say the group of words and keep them lifted as you say them. Feel as if the sounds were floating up freely and easily. Don't try to force them up.

Most students make a little too much effort at first when they say the questions, just as beginners do when they first try to hit a golf ball or a tennis ball. This may make your voice go a little too high as you say the questions at first. However, as you keep on trying, with your cheeks lifted and feeling as if the sounds you are making were floating up freely and easily, without any force, your voice will gradually adjust itself to its own proper muscle level.

MY NAME IS - - - -

After you have said "See Me Please" with the questions for a while and it begins to feel easy to do, try saying your name in the same way.

Keep your cheeks lifted as in the picture for the cheek muscle exercise and say each word as if you were asking a question, like this:

My? Name? Is? (Your first name)? (Your last name)?

As you have been doing with "See Me Please", be sure to lift your cheeks as in the picture for the cheek muscle exercise each time before you say the words. Keep them lifted as you say them. Again, give the sounds plenty of time to float up. Don't try to force or push them up. Just feel as if they were floating up freely and easily by themselves.

Do these exercises any time you think of them. As with the muscle exercise, don't make a job of them. Have fun with them. They will help give you the feeling of what your voice should be like. It is the beginning of a live and resonant voice for you, one that can be heard easily and that will be listened to whenever you have something to say.

READING ALOUD

After you have become familiar with saying words as if you were asking questions, then try reading aloud.

As shown in the portion of the *Gettysburg Address* which follows, break the reading material up into short phrases and feel as if you were asking a question with each phrase.

Try reading the portion of the *Gettysburg Address* again. Read it in short phrases as indicated by the question marks. Say each phrase as if you were asking a question. Keep your cheeks lifted and feel that the sounds are floating up freely and easily. Don't force them up. Let them float up by themselves.

Four score? and seven years ago? our fathers brought forth? upon this continent? a new nation? conceived in liberty? and dedicated? to the proposition? that all men? are created equal?

Now we are engaged? in a great civil war? testing whether that nation? or any nation? so conceived? and so dedicated? can long endure?

We are met? on a great battle field? of that war? We have

come to dedicate? a portion of that field? as a final resting place? for those? who here gave their lives? that that nation? might live? It is altogether fitting? and proper? that we should do this?

Don't read too rapidly. Give the sounds plenty of time to float up.

After you have read the portion of the *Gettysburg Address* with the questions a few times and it begins to feel easy to do, make a second recording, reading the portion given with the questions indicated.

Then play your first recording and then this one. If you have followed through carefully as instructed, you should hear more resonance and quality in your voice in the second recording. This is because your voice is beginning to be on its own proper muscle level and the vibrations of the sounds you are making are beginning to float up to the resonating material of the top of your head.

After you have practiced reading this portion of the *Gettysburg Address* for a while, try reading the rest of it in the same manner. Also try reading in this way from newspapers, articles, books, any material you may have at hand. If you use your voice professionally, practice reading your radio or TV script, your lecture or your sermon this way.

As you read along, break each sentence into phrases of a few words each and read each phrase as if you were asking a question, just as you have been doing with the *Gettysburg Address*.

This is all of the material for your first lesson; the exercises for the muscles of your cheeks, "See Me Please", saying your name and reading as if you were asking questions.

Read the material given in the chapter carefully. Study the pictures and do the exercises as instructed and have fun with all of them.

In the next chapter you will learn about another part of your vocal instrument, how to say some more sounds and how to begin using your voice correctly in your daily conversation.

Chapter Five

THE NOSE

BY THE TIME you begin this chapter you should be able to move your cheeks up and down quite easily. Always remember to concentrate on the muscles high up under your eyes and let them do all of the work for you. As you continue to do the exercise, you should feel as if the lift extended back to your ears, as if it took in the entire top of your head.

It should also be easy for you to use the lift of your cheek muscles when you are saying "See Me Please" and your name. As you continue to say them, feel as if you could sustain the vowel sounds for a longer period of time. It takes additional muscle strength to sustain the vowel sounds. The additional muscle strength you gain by sustaining them easily helps in strengthening your vocal instrument for use in speaking and singing.

You should be feeling that your voice is floating up freely and easily as you read with the questions. There is no better practice for feeling the proper muscle level for your speaking voice than reading with the questions.

This time you will become acquainted with the muscles of your nose.

The muscles of the nose must be loose and free so that they can lift simultaneously with the lift of the muscles of the cheeks. This lift allows the nasal passages to remain open and permits the air to flow freely through them.

Any tension in the muscles of the nose interferes with the lift of the muscles of the cheeks and closes in on the nasal passages. I have had cases where the vocal disability was mainly due to the patient's habit of tensing and pulling down the muscles of his nose when trying to force the air or voice out.

The following exercise will help you keep the muscles of your nose loose and free.

17

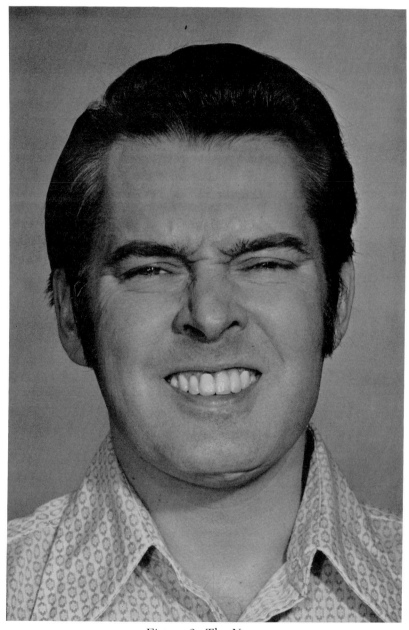

Figure 3. The Nose

Take your mirror and look at the bridge of your nose. This is the part between your eyes.

Try to wrinkle up the muscles of the bridge of your nose as if you were trying to push off a pair of spectacles as shown in Figure 3.

Be sure that your lips are apart.

Hold them a moment.

Let go of them.

Wrinkle them up again.

Hold them.

Let go of them.

Wrinkle them up.

Let go of them.

Don't do the exercise too rapidly. Hold the muscles a short time each time you wrinkle them up. If you do it too rapidly, you will not get the full benefit of the exercise.

Practice wrinkling up the bridge of your nose whenever you think of it. If you have any difficulty doing it at first, keep at it and in a short time you will be able to do it very easily. I have had many students who could not move the muscles of their noses at all at first.

You must concentrate on the bridge of your nose and feel that those muscles are doing all of the work by themselves. When they are properly exercised, and are loose and free, you don't have to think about the muscles of your nose when you are speaking or singing. They follow along with the lift of the muscles of the cheeks.

THE S SOUNDS—S-Z SH-ZH CH-J

This time you will learn how to say the S Sounds correctly.

There are six of these sounds, S as in Snake, Z as in Zebra, SH as in SHake, ZH as in MeaSure, CH as in CHair and J as in Jar.

I refer to them as the S Sounds merely because they all follow through with a muscle usage similar to that used for saying the sound of S. The cheeks are lifted and the air flows freely and easily against the upper edges of the upper teeth.

You can get this feeling by lifting your cheeks and hissing like a snake.

You cannot produce an S Sound correctly without having the muscles of your cheeks lifted. When your cheeks are lifted, your tongue can go where it is supposed to go and the air can go where it is supposed to go.

To get used to saying them correctly, practice saying the following sets of words.

Keep your cheeks lifted high up under your eyes as shown in the picture for the cheek muscle exercise.

Say each word as if you were asking a question, just as you have been doing with "See Me Please" and saying your name.

Seal?	Sail?	Sell?
Zeal?	Zail?	Zell?
SHeal?	SHail?	SHell?
ZHeal?	ZHail?	ZHell?
CHeal?	CHail?	CHell?
Jeal?	Jail?	Jell?

Let all of the sounds float up freely and easily.

If you are having difficulty with any of these sounds, practicing them this way will help you say them correctly.

YOUR DAILY CONVERSATION
—begins on next page

Figure 4. A Pleasant Smile or Expression

YOUR DAILY CONVERSATION

The most important thing for you, of course, is to begin to use your vocal instrument and your voice correctly in your daily conversation, whether at home or in your business or profession. You can begin to help yourself right away.

All you have to do is to feel that you have a pleasant smile or expression on your face and that your voice is floating up freely and easily. Figure 2, for the cheek muscle exercise, shows the exaggerated lift we use for practice. When speaking in our daily conversation we use an easy, gentle lift that just gives us a pleasant smile or expression as in Figure 4.

Be sure you smile with your cheeks and not with your lips. A smile should always feel as if it were coming from the lift of the muscles up under your eyes. This smile gives you the feeling of the lift of your cheeks. The idea of your voice floating up freely and easily begins to keep it on its proper muscle level.

For practice you can use the smile and questions over the telephone without anyone seeing you or thinking anything of it. Say "Hello? Mrs. Smith speaking?" I always stress this particularly with those who have to answer the telephone all day in offices. You do not have to exaggerate the questions, but just the idea of it will keep your voice up on its own proper muscle level. Whether you are answering the telephone at your work or at home, it's a good way to remind yourself of what you should be doing with your muscles and your voice.

You cannot always be thinking about what you are doing with your face and your voice when you are talking to someone but you can remind yourself about it occasionally until the correct usage becomes habit.

If the muscles of your cheeks have sagged a great deal or have not been used at all, you may feel a bit self-conscious about smiling at first. Many students do. However, after trying to speak with a pleasant smile or expression for a while it feels perfectly easy and natural. It is the natural way to speak. The old, lifeless expression, which may feel natural to you now, and the voice that goes with it, is the unnatural one.

As you get used to using your muscles and your voice this way, you will find that you'll look better and you'll sound better. Your face will make much more of an impression on your listeners and so will your voice. You will find that you'll be understood more easily and that people will pay much more attention to what you have to say.

Watch what happens to you, to your face, and to your voice. You will probably have friends remarking about how much better you are looking and they may not recognize your voice over the telephone. It is always interesting to listen to reactions like these from students as they continue to work and improve.

This time you have two new exercises, the one for your nose and the other for the S Sounds. Don't forget to keep doing the exercises for your cheeks, "See Me Please", your name and reading with the questions. Reading with the questions gives you the feeling of the way you should begin using your voice in your daily conversation.

Try speaking with a pleasant smile or expression on your face and the feeling that your voice is floating up freely and easily. When you speak this way you are practicing correctly with every sound you make.

Chapter Six

THE LIPS

THE MUSCLES OF your nose should now be loose and free and you should be able to wrinkle up the bridge quite easily. Always remember to concentrate on the bridge of your nose and to leave your lips apart.

You should also be able to say the S Sounds correctly and easily with your cheeks lifted and the air flowing freely and easily against the upper edges of your teeth. When you say them this way, your tongue can go where it is supposed to go and the air can go where it is supposed to go.

If you have been taking some time each day to read aloud as if you were asking questions, your voice should be becoming stronger and more resonant. Be sure to let the sounds of the questions float up freely and easily.

This time you will learn about your lips.

The muscles of the lips must be soft and pliable so that they, too, can lift along with the lift of the muscles of the cheeks.

Many persons cover their teeth with their lips when speaking because of self-consciousness over dental irregularities, discolored teeth, dentures or bands. They do not realize that even if there is a slight defect, the full flash of the upper teeth and the attractive facial expression that goes with it makes the defect itself practically unnoticeable.

Covering the teeth with the lips interferes with the lift of the muscles of the cheeks and the flow of air through the oral cavity. They must never be held over the teeth.

I have had many cases of ailments of the larynx referred to me where the ailment was entirely due to holding the upper lip over the upper teeth. In many cases the muscles of the lips had become so stiffened and tensed that the patient could not do the simple, childlike exercises I use for the lip muscles.

We use the following exercise for the muscles of the lips. Doing this exercise will keep your lips soft and pliable and ready for saying correctly the consonant sounds you make with your lips.

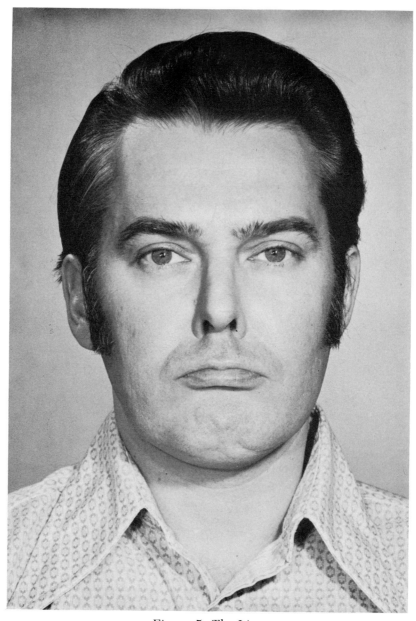

Figure 5. The Lips

Take your mirror and look at your lips.

Try to pout them as shown in Figure 5.

Let your lips feel soft, as if there were no muscles in them.

Feel that the sides of your face are soft and puffing out with your lips.

When they really do feel soft, try blowing air through them, making them vibrate loosely and freely as a horse does when he sneezes.

Again, feel as if the sides of your face were puffing out with your lips.

It is a simple exercise. However, unless you can make them vibrate freely and easily, your lip muscles are not ready to use correctly when you speak or sing.

If your lips have been held very tightly, you may not be able to make them vibrate at all at first. I have had many students who could not. Some have to practice for several weeks before their lips begin to vibrate. However, as you continue to try, the tight and constricted muscles will gradually let go and you will be able to do the exercise easily.

THE LIP SOUNDS

WH-W M-P-B F-V

After you have tried the exercise for your lips for a while and they begin to feel soft and pliable, try the following three sets of exercises for the consonant sounds you make with your lips.

There are seven of these sounds: *WH* as in WHither, *W* as in Wither, *M* as in Man, *P* as in Pan, *B* as in Ban, *F* as in Fan and *V* as in Van.

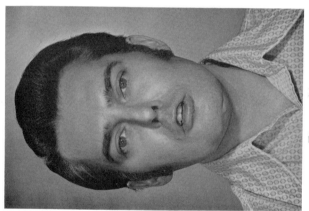

Figure 6A.

WH . . . .

Figure 6B.

. . . . . . ither

WH-W

First try saying the *WH* and *W* sounds.

When you say these sounds, pout your lips softly and keep them slightly parted as in Figure 6A on the left.

Then let them spring quickly and easily away to the lift of your cheek muscles for the sounds that follow, as in Figure 6B on the right.

Say each of the following sets of words this way, saying each word as if you were asking a question:

WHither?	WHether?	WHence?
Wither?	Wether?	Wence?

Keep on saying them this way until you can spring quickly and easily from the pout to the lift of your cheek muscles.

This exercise in springing to the lift of the cheek muscles is especially good for you if you have not been using your cheeks very much when you speak.

Figure 7A. M . . . . an Figure 7B.

M-P-B

Now try saying the *M*, *P* and *B* sounds.

When you say these sounds, pout your lips softly as in Figure 7 A on the left.

Then let them spring quickly and easily away to the lift of your cheek muscles for the sounds that follow, just as you have been doing for the *WH* and *W* sounds, as in Figure 7B on the right.

Say each of the following sets of words this way, saying each word as if you were asking a question:

Man?	Men?	Mean?
Pan?	Pen?	Pean?
Ban?	Ben?	Bean?

Keep on saying them this way until you can spring quickly and easily from your pouted lips to the lift of your cheek muscles.

Figure 8A.

Figure 8B.

F . . . . an

F-V

The last two Lip Sounds are the sounds of *F* and *V*.

When you say these sounds you use only your lower lip.

Lift your cheeks and let your lower lip touch your upper teeth lightly as in Figure 8A on the left.

Then blow your lower lip softly away from your upper teeth as you say the *F* and *V* sounds.

Let your cheeks remain lifted for the sounds that follow, as in Figure 8B on the right.

Say each of the following sets of words this way, saying each word as if you were asking a question:

Fan?	Fen?	Fean?
Van?	Ven?	Vean?

Keep on saying them this way until your lower lip feels soft when you blow it away.

Now you have learned how to exercise your lip muscles correctly and how to use them correctly when you make the Lip Sounds. These are your new exercises for this time.

Don't forget to keep up your cheek and nose exercises. Keep on saying the *S* Sounds, "See Me Please", your name and reading with the questions.

Keep on using a pleasant smile in your daily conversation and feel as if the sounds you are making were floating up freely and easily. In this way you are practicing correctly every time you talk to someone.

Your daily conversation is your practice.

Chapter Seven

THE LOWER JAW

Y OUR LIPS SHOULD now be able to vibrate freely and easily when you blow the air through them. They should also be able to spring quickly and easily to the lift of your cheek muscles when you say the Lip Sounds.

The important thing to remember is that you should never hold your upper lip over your teeth when you are speaking or singing. Your upper teeth should always be in view excepting, of course, for the brief moments you pout them when you say the Lip Sounds. If you hold your lips over your teeth, neither the consonant sounds you make with your lips nor the vowel sounds that follow them can be said correctly.

This time you will learn about your lower jaw.

The muscles which move the lower jaw must be loose and free. The lower jaw must have the ability to adjust quickly in opening and closing the mouth when helping to form the various vowel and consonant sounds.

When the muscles of the lower jaw are tense and constricted, they cause the lower jaw to be held tightly. Holding the lower jaw tightly closes in on the room inside the mouth which is necessary for resonating the vowel sounds.

I have had cases of vocal disabilities where this tension not only caused the ailment of the larynx but also extreme tension in the back of the neck and habitual grinding of the teeth. I had a case at one time where the teeth had been ground down so badly that it was necessary to have them capped. I have had cases referred to me where stiffened muscles that move the lower jaw have been entirely responsible for the vocal disability.

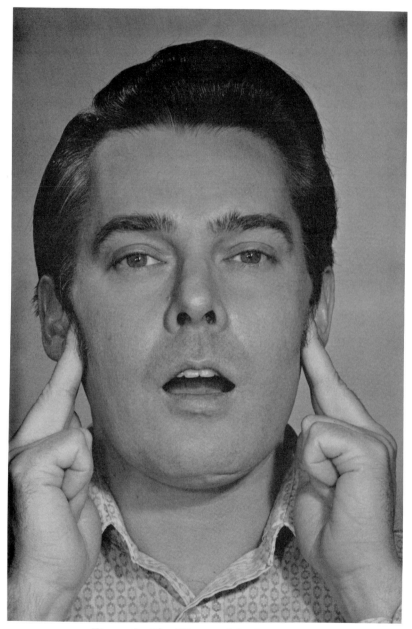

Figure 9. The Hinges of the Lower Jaw

If you will put the tips of your index and middle fingers of each hand in front of the lower parts of your ears and move your lower jaw up and down, as in Figure 9, you will feel the muscles that move it up and down. I usually refer to them as the muscles that move the hinges of the lower jaw.

These muscles must always be loose and free so that your lower jaw can move up and down loosely and freely.

Now that you know where they are, doing the following exercise will help you keep them loose and free.

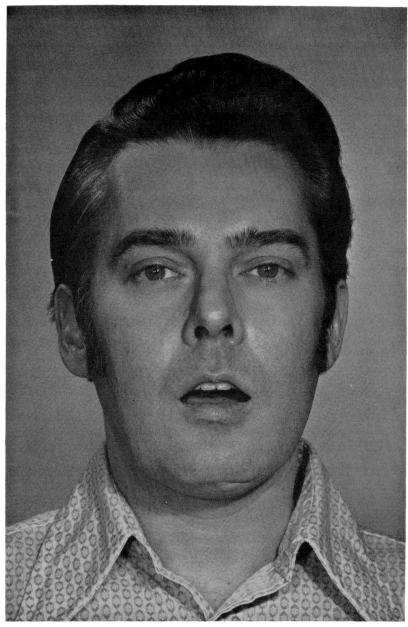

Figure 10. The Lower Jaw

Look in your mirror.

Let your lower jaw drop slowly and gently on its hinges, as in Figure 10.

Feel as if it were so heavy that it could drop onto the floor of its own weight.

Let the muscles in front of your ears feel soft and loose.

Now close your jaw slowly and gently.

Let it drop slowly again, as if it were dropping of its own weight.

Close it slowly and gently.

Let it drop.

Close it.

Don't try to force or push it down.

Feel as if it were dropping of its own weight.

Keep on dropping and closing it until the muscles feel loose and free. You should have a feeling of softness in the muscles of the side of your face (those in front of your ears) as you move your jaw up and down.

For those whose jaws are particularly tense and who have a habit of grinding their teeth at night, I always recommend that they do the exercise just before going to sleep. This helps to keep them from becoming tense and clenched during the night.

When you speak and sing you should feel as if your lower jaw were dropping gently on its hinges, almost as if it were dropping back under your ears. Don't try to pull or push it back. Just let it drop by itself. This feeling lets your muscles drop loosely and freely, with no tension. Thrusting the lower jaw forward, which is a common fault with singers, causes the muscles to become tense and constricted.

SOME MISCELLANEOUS CONSONANT SOUNDS

K-G H Y R NG

This time you will learn how to say some miscellaneous consonant sounds.

These are all of the consonant sounds that are not included in the S Sounds, the Lip Sounds and the Tongue Sounds, which you will learn about next time.

There are six of these sounds, K as in Kale, G as in Gale, H as in Hat, Y as in Yet and R and NG as in RiNG.

When you say these sounds you lift the muscles of your cheeks and feel as if the sounds were floating up freely and easily.

Say the following sets of words this way, saying each word as if you were asking a question.

Keep your cheeks lifted as shown in the picture for the cheek exercise.

Feel as if each of the sounds were floating up freely and easily.

Keel?	Kale?	Call?
Geel?	Gale?	Gall?
Heel?	Hale?	Hall?
Yeel?	Yale?	Yall?
RiNG?	RaNG?	RuNG?

Be sure that your cheeks remain lifted on the last word of each group. Most people are inclined to drop their cheeks on the *AW* and *UH* sounds.

Keep on saying them until you do feel that they are all floating up freely and easily.

This time you have the new exercises for your lower jaw and the miscellaneous consonant sounds to practice.

While you are adding these new exercises, be sure to keep on doing all of your previous ones.

Again, keep a pleasant smile on your face and feel that the sounds you are making are floating up freely and easily in your reading and in your daily conversation.

Chapter Eight

THE TONGUE

A FTER DOING THE exercise for the muscles that move the hinges of your lower jaw, you should have the feeling that your lower jaw is moving up and down loosely and freely. The important thing to remember is that these muscles must feel soft and loose when you are doing the exercise and when you are speaking and singing.

You should also be able to do the exercises for the miscellaneous consonant sounds with your cheeks lifted and the feeling that the sounds are floating up. Remember to keep your cheeks lifted when you say the *AW* and *UH* sounds as in Call and Rung.

You have now learned about the muscles of your face that are important to your speaking and singing: those of your cheeks, nose, lips and lower jaw. This time you will go inside your mouth and learn about your tongue.

Your tongue can be a very unruly member of your vocal instrument unless you treat it properly. If there is any tension in its muscles you cannot say or sing your vowel and consonant sounds correctly.

It must always lie softly in its groove of saliva. Then, when all of the other muscles of your vocal instrument are used correctly, it has the ability to move about gently and easily as it should when helping to form the various vowel and consonant sounds.

The following exercises will help you to soften the muscles of your tongue and get them ready for you to use correctly when you speak and sing.

41

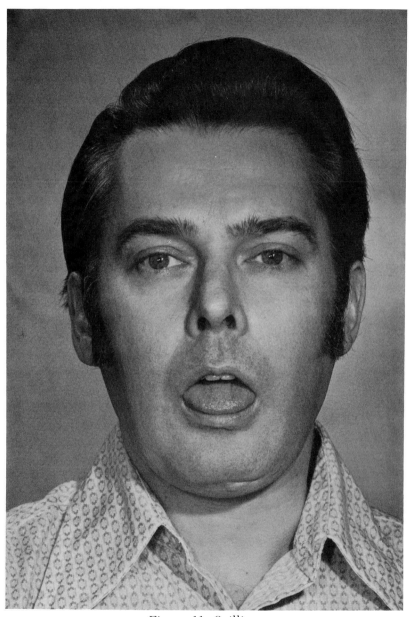

Figure 11. Spilling

The first exercise we use is to help you to soften the muscles of your tongue and get rid of any tension in them.

This exercise we call Spilling.

Take a mirror and look at your face.

Drop your lower jaw loosely and freely as you are doing in the exercise for the muscles of the hinges of your lower jaw. This should now be easy for you to do.

As you drop your jaw, let your tongue spill softly out of your mouth as shown in Figure 11.

Feel as if the front end of it were so heavy that it could fall onto the floor of its own weight.

Don't try to force or push it out.

Just let it hang there loosely and freely until you do have the feeling of its being soft and loose. Let it feel as if it had not a muscle in it.

When you get this feeling of softness, you will notice that the front end of your tongue is loose and rounded, as shown in Figure 11.

It is this loose rounded front end of your tongue that you use when you say the consonant sounds you make with your tongue.

The following two exercises will show you how to exercise this loose rounded front end of your tongue correctly and get it ready for saying the Tongue Sounds correctly.

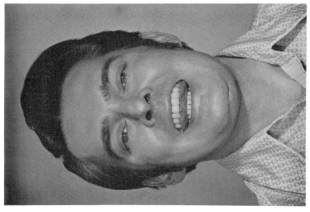

Figure 12A.   Licking   Figure 12B.

The first exercise we do for the loose rounded front end of the tongue we call Licking.

Take your mirror and look at your face.

Lift the muscles of your cheeks and let your lower jaw drop loosely and freely.

Now lick the front of the roof of your mouth gently with the front of your tongue.

Lick gently forward, letting your tongue lick the backs of your upper front teeth, as shown in Figure 12A on the left.

Then let it spill gently out of your mouth, just as you did for the Spilling exercise, as in Figure 12B on the right.

Practice Licking, slowly and gently, until the front end of your tongue spills softly and easily out of your mouth.

Be sure that your tongue feels soft when it is moving.

It is this feeling of softness when it's moving that is important.

Figure 13A.

Figure 13B.

Lapping

The second exercise for the front of the tongue we call Lapping.

It is just the opposite of Licking.

Take your mirror again and look at your face.

Lift the muscles of your cheeks gently and let your lower jaw drop loosely and freely.

Pretend to lap up some milk out of a saucer, like a kitten.

Start with the loose, rounded front end of your tongue spilled out of your mouth, as you did for the Spilling exercise, as in Figure 13A on the left.

Then let it lap gently backward into your mouth, as in Figure 13B on the right.

Let it touch the lower edges of your upper teeth lightly as it goes into your mouth.

Keep on Lapping, slowly and gently, until your tongue feels soft when it is lapping.

You must always have this feeling of softness in your tongue when it's moving, when you are doing the exercise and when you are speaking and singing.

THE TONGUE SOUNDS

L-N-T-D TH-TH

After you have exercised the front end of your tongue for a while and it feels soft and loose when you are Licking and Lapping, try the following three sets of exercises for the consonant sounds which you make with your tongue.

There are six of these sounds, *L* as in Lie, *N* as in Nigh, *T* as in Tie, *D* as in Die, *TH* as in THigh and *TH* as in THy.

When you say the *L, N, T* and *D* sounds, the loose, rounded front end of your tongue waves gently up and down at the front of your mouth behind your front teeth.

When you say the two *TH* sounds, it waves gently backward from between your teeth.

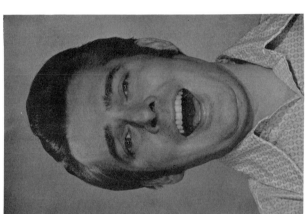

Figure 14A.

Figure 14B.

L . . . . ah

To get used to waving your tongue on the Tongue Sounds, lift your cheeks and try saying Lah-Lah-Lah-Lah-Lah? as if you were asking a question, repeating it many times.

Figure 14A on the left shows the tongue at the beginning of the L sound, 14B on the right shows it after the sound has been said.

Let your tongue wave gently up and down when you say the L sounds.

Be sure to keep your cheeks lifted while you say them.

As you get used to the waving, see that your lower jaw does not wave up and down with your tongue. Don't try to make your lower jaw stay still. Just let it hang there. Most people move their lower jaws up and down with their tongues when they begin. Your tongue should do all of the waving by itself.

Keep on saying the groups of Lah's until the waving feels free and easy.

Figure 15A. L

Figure 15B. .... ie

When it has become easy for you to wave your tongue up and down when saying Lah, try saying the sounds of *L, N, T* and *D.*

When you say these sounds you lift the muscles of your cheeks and wave your tongue gently up and down at the front of your mouth, behind your front teeth, just as you have been doing with Lah-Lah-Lah.

Figure 15A on the left shows the tongue when beginning the *L* sound, 15B on the right shows it lying softly in the mouth after the *L* sound has been said.

Say each of the following sets of words this way, saying each word as if you were asking a question:

Lie?	Lay?	Lain?
Nie?	Nay?	Nain?
Tie?	Tay?	Tain?
Die?	Day?	Dain?

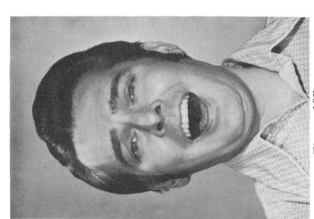

Figure 16A. . . . . Figure 16B.

TH . . . . igh

As you keep on saying the words, be sure your cheeks are lifted and your tongue is waving up and down gently and easily.

Now try the other two Tongue Sounds, the sou ds of *TH* as in THigh and T.Iy.

When you say these sounds, lift your cheeks and wave your tongue gently backward from between your teeth.

Figure 16A on the left shows the tongue at the beginning of the sound, the front end lying softly between the teeth. Figure 16B on the right shows it lying softly in the mouth after the TH sound has been said.

Say each of the following sets of words this way, saying each word as if you were asking a question:

THigh? THay? THane?
THy? THey? THain?

As you keep on saying them, be sure that your cheeks are lifted and that your tongue is waving backward gently and easily.

When two Tongue Sounds come together, we make only one waving motion of the tongue for the two sounds, as in las*t n*ight, mi*dn*ight, brigh*tn*ess. Practice saying these combinations and any other combinations of two Tongue Sounds you come across in your reading this way, with only one waving motion of your tongue.

This waving motion when you say the Tongue Sounds is the only thing you ever ask your tongue to do. On all other sounds it should lie softly in your mouth in its groove of saliva, as if about to spill out over your lower front teeth.

When you let it lie softly in its groove of saliva and use all of the other muscles of your vocal instrument correctly when you speak and sing, your tongue will then do what it is supposed to do when helping to form the various vowel and consonant sounds.

If you have been reading with the questions and have been using a smile or pleasant expression in your daily conversation, you should now be able to read and speak without thinking of the questions.

Try reading the *Gettysburg Address* and any other material you have at hand without using the questions this time.

Your voice should now be staying on its proper muscle level. It should feel as if the sounds you are making were floating from your ears up. Your voice should be going up and down easily in pitch as you express yourself without dropping down muscularly. Speaking on your own correct muscle level should be your habit now and any old incorrect habits should have gone away.

If you do feel yourself dropping down muscularly or if you feel any discomfort when reading or speaking, this will tell you that you have gone back toward your old habits for a moment. When this happens, think of the questions again until you get on your own correct muscle level. It is a good idea to read with the questions at times just to remind yourself of what you should be doing.

Read both ways this time, both with and without the questions.

Concentrate particularly on your tongue exercises this time. You should take plenty of time to get acquainted with your tongue. It is a very important and, as we have said, often a very unruly member of your vocal instrument.

And don't forget to do all of your other exercises.

Chapter Nine

THE SOFT PALATE

Your tongue should now feel soft and loose when you do your Licking and Lapping exercises. It should feel as if it had not a muscle in it. It should also be able to wave gently up and down when you say the Tongue Sounds.

The important thing to remember about your tongue is that the only thing you ever ask it to do is to wave gently up and down when you say the Tongue Sounds. The rest of the time it should lie softly in its groove of saliva in your mouth, as if it were about to spill out over your lower front teeth. It will then do whatever it is supposed to do when you are speaking and singing, provided, of course, that you are using all of the other muscles of your vocal instrument correctly.

This time you will learn about your soft palate and the room you have inside your mouth.

The muscles of the soft palate must be correctly strengthened so that it can lift automatically along with the lift of the muscles of the cheeks. It is this lift of the soft palate, together with the loose drop of the lower jaw, that forms the room inside the mouth necessary for resonating the vowel sounds.

This room inside the mouth is necessary when using full voice, as when speaking over loud sounds or noise, in a large room or auditorium, in the theatre and when singing.

Using insufficient room inside the mouth is one of the main causes of difficulties singers have in producing vowel sounds, especially on the higher tones. It has also been the main cause of ailments of the larynx in persons referred to me for vocal disabilities due to speaking over loud sounds or noise and in children referred because of ailments of the larynx due to shouting at games and on playgrounds.

In order to become acquainted with your own soft palate, take your mirror and look at the inside of your mouth. At the back you will see the arch of your soft palate with the uvula hanging down in the center.

Figure 17. The Arch of the Hollywood Bowl

Now look at Figure 17.

It is a picture of the arch of the Hollywood Bowl I took many years ago when visiting in Hollywood. I always use it in my studio to illustrate the arch inside the mouth and its usage. You will notice that the inside of your mouth is shaped exactly like it. It resonates and projects the sounds of the musical instruments and singers just as the room inside your mouth resonates and projects the sounds of your voice.

If the muscles of your soft palate are collapsed or sagging, they close in on this room inside your mouth and dull the vibrations of your voice. They must be strengthened correctly so that they can lift automatically as you lift the muscles of your cheeks.

Doing the exercise which follows will help strengthen them for you.

Figure 18. The Soft Palate

Take your mirror.

Lift your cheeks and let your lower jaw drop loosely and freely as you open your mouth.

Now yawn, gently and easily, as in Figure 18.

The arch of your soft palate will lift as you yawn.

If you would like to see how it lifts, take a look at it in your mirror. It is not necessary to look at it as you continue to practice yawning. It will lift as you yawn.

Hold it a moment.

Let it drop.

Yawn again, gently and easily.

Hold it a moment.

Let it drop.

Yawn again.

Hold it.

Let it drop.

As you practice yawning, you will no doubt feel that you are really beginning to yawn. When you do, don't stop it. Have a big yawn and stretch for yourself. There is nothing better for the muscles of the inside of your mouth than a yawn. It's like giving them all a good massage.

As you continue to practice yawning, be sure to see that your cheeks are lifted gently. It won't do you any good to yawn with your cheeks dropped. Your soft palate won't lift and you won't feel the room at the back of your mouth.

Then be sure that your lower jaw is dropped loosely and freely of its own weight, as if it were just hanging there.

And finally, after you have become accustomed to yawning with your cheeks lifted and your lower jaw dropped loosely, see that your tongue is lying softly in your mouth as you yawn, as if about to spill out over your lower front teeth.

Eventually you should be able to do all three of these things automatically as you yawn. Your cheeks will be lifted gently, your lower jaw dropped loosely and freely and your tongue lying softly in your mouth, as if about to spill out over your lower front teeth.

When your soft palate is properly strengthened through yawning correctly, it will lift automatically along with the lift of your cheeks when you are speaking and singing.

Never try to lift your soft palate voluntarily when you are speaking or singing. If you do, you will tense muscles which should be loose and free.

THE AH SOUNDS
—begins on next page

Figure 19. How AH . . re You?

After you have practiced yawning for a while and you have felt the room inside your mouth, try using it when you make sounds.

Try saying "How Are You?"

Lift your cheeks gently and see that your lower jaw is dropped loosely and freely.

Then say "How Are You?" as shown in Figure 19.

Feel as if you were just saying *AH* instead of Are.

Prolong and sustain the *AH* sound in Are.

Let it fill up the room inside the arch at the back of your mouth. Feel as if you had a mouthful of sound. Feel as if the sounds were floating up and out of the back of your head.

Keep on saying "How Are You?" this way until you do feel as if you had a mouthful of *AH* sounds floating freely and easily up and out of the arch of the back of your head, as if floating up and out of your ears.

THE AH SOUNDS

When you have become used to feeling the *AH* sounds filling up the room inside your mouth, try saying other words with the sound of *AH* in them.

Say the following words with *AH* in them, saying each word as if you were asking a question.

OW is *AH* plus $\overline{OO}$. I is *AH* plus $\overline{E}$. Say them as if they were *AH*'s with only a little $\overline{OO}$ or $\overline{E}$ at the end.

Remember to lift your cheeks and let your lower jaw hang loosely and freely as you say them.

Bough?	Now?	Chow?	Cow?
Might?	Light?	Sight?	Kite?
What?	Dot?	Shot?	Got?

Sustain and prolong the *AH* sound in each word, almost as if you were singing it.

Let all of the *AH* sounds float up freely and easily into the arch at the back of your mouth. Feel as if they were floating up and out of the back of your head, as if they were floating up and out of your ears.

This room inside the mouth, at the back of the mouth, can

not be emphasized too much. You should always feel as if the sounds of your voice were floating up back of your molars, back of where the hinges of your lower jaw are dropped loosely. You should feel as if the sounds were floating up and out of the back of your head, as if they were floating up and out of your ears. This use of the room at the back of your mouth lets the sounds you make grow in resonance, volume and quality.

You must never try to project your voice or have the feeling that you are making the sounds come forward. This can tense and constrict your muscles and make your voice grow smaller. When you use the room inside your mouth correctly, your vocal instrument projects the sounds of your voice for you.

After you have practiced the words in the exercises for a while, say other words with the sounds of *AH*, *OW* and *I* in them, such as Round, Sound, Mound, White, Night, Right, saying them as if you were asking questions. The old phrase, "How now, brown cow?", is a good one for practice.

By this time you should be able to stay on your own correct muscle level when you are reading without using the questions. The feeling when you are speaking on your own correct muscle level is that your voice is floating freely and easily from your ears up.

READING AND SPEAKING IN FULL VOICE

When you have accomplished speaking on your own correct muscle level and you feel that your voice is floating freely and easily from your ears up, then you can begin to read and speak with more volume.

Practice reading as if you were reading to someone across the room from you or outside the window. Be sure to keep your cheeks lifted and to feel that you have plenty of room inside your mouth. Let the sounds you are making fill up this room inside your mouth and feel as if they were floating from your ears up.

Read this way for only a short time at first. Then, as your voice feels stronger and more resonant, you can read this way for longer intervals. Always stop if you feel the least bit tired.

When you read and speak with more volume, don't try to force or push the sounds out. Just let them float up as you have been doing all along in your reading. You just feel as if more air were floating up. Your muscles must feel just as soft and loose and free when you are speaking loudly as when you are speaking softly. You just feel as if there were more sound floating up into the arch at the back of your mouth.

READING AND SPEAKING SOFTLY

When you speak softly you must have the feeling that you are staying on the same muscle level as when you are speaking loudly. You feel as if your voice were floating from your ears up.

Most people have difficulty at first when speaking softly, as when speaking over the telephone or to someone near them. Instead of keeping on their correct muscle level they drop onto their throats. You must feel that you are staying on the same muscle level that you have been using when reading and speaking in your normal voice.

Try reading softly with the questions until you have the feeling that your voice is floating from your ears up. Then read and speak without the questions but with the same feeling of your voice floating up.

WHISPERING

When you whisper you must also feel that you are staying on your correct muscle level. The whisper must feel as if it, too, were floating freely and easily from your ears up.

A whisper that is produced incorrectly muscularly can cause a strain on the muscles of the larynx and vocal cords. It is of no use to tell a person to whisper in order to protect his throat unless you show him how to whisper correctly muscularly. I only use the whisper with persons referred by their physicians when it is too painful for them to speak in a normal voice at first. However, we should all know how to whisper correctly, particularly an actor in the theatre whose audience must be able to hear what he is saying.

Try reading in a whisper, using the questions and letting the whisper float up freely and easily. Then read and speak in a whisper without using the questions but feeling that the sounds are floating freely and easily from your ears up.

For this time concentrate particularly on yawning and using the room inside your mouth correctly when you say "How Are You?" and the words with the *AH* sounds in them. This is the room that lets your voice grow in resonance, richness, volume and beauty; so spend plenty of time learning how to use it correctly.

Also spend some time reading with more volume, in full voice, reading and speaking softly, and whispering.

Chapter Ten

THE WAIST

IF YOU HAVE FOLLOWED through correctly with the instructions in the previous lesson, you should now be able to yawn correctly with your cheeks lifted, your lower jaw dropped loosely and freely and your tongue lying softly in your mouth, as if about to spill out over your lower front teeth.

These are the three important things to remember when you are yawning and using the room in the arch at the back of your mouth. They will all happen for you automatically as you continue to practice yawning correctly.

You should now be able to use this room at the back of your mouth correctly when you say "How Are You?" and when saying the words with the *AH* sounds in them.

You should also be able to read and speak in full voice, softly, and in a whisper on your own correct muscle level without causing any strain on the muscles of your larynx or vocal cords.

This time you will learn about the muscles of your waist.

These are the muscles which, when properly strengthened and used, help to keep your body in proper alignment or posture.

If they are sagging or collapsed, the body is thrown out of alignment and the air or breath cannot flow freely in and out as it should.

The muscles of the waist must be correctly strengthened so that they can remain drawn in gently and easily at all times when speaking and singing.

The next exercise will help strengthen them for you.

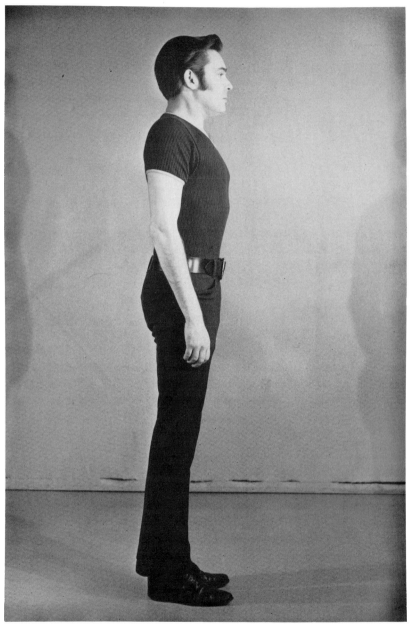

Figure 20. The Waist

Draw in the muscles at your waist, where your belt buckle would be, gently and easily, as shown in Figure 20.

Hold them a moment.

Let go of them.

Draw them in again, gently and easily.

Let them go.

Draw them in.

Let them go.

Don't do the exercise too many times at first.

If you have not been using or exercising these muscles very much, the exercise may make your back ache at first.

Do it gently and easily and then gradually increase the number of times you do it as muscle strength comes in.

ALIGNMENT OR POSTURE

If you will stand sidewise in front of a mirror and look at yourself as you gently and easily draw in the muscles of your waist, you will see your entire body come into proper alignment. Your waist will draw in, your chest and shoulders will rise and your back will straighten.

In order to keep your body in proper alignment or posture you should see that these muscles at your waist are always drawn in gently and easily when you are sitting as well as when you are standing. It is especially important when sitting as most of us are inclined to let these muscles slump when we sit. I have to stress this particularly with those who sit in offices and talk to people during the day. Any slump or other muscle usage that throws the body out of alignment places a strain on the muscles of the throat.

When you are speaking or singing, always see that your feet are firmly planted on the floor when you're standing or that you are firmly seated on your chair when sitting; and that the muscles at your waist are drawn in gently and easily.

Then see that the muscles of your chest and shoulders are loose and free. There must never be any tension in them such as happens when you pull your shoulders back. They must always be able to move about freely and easily.

Then you must see that the muscles of your neck are also loose and free, as if your head could nod gently and easily, as if it could spill onto the floor of its own weight.

The support for your vocal instrument is from your feet to your waist. The upper part of your instrument, your chest, shoulders, neck and head, must be as loose and free as a rag doll's so that your air or breath can flow freely and easily in and out of you.

BREATHING

When your entire body, which is your entire vocal instrument, is in proper alignment and all of its muscles are used correctly, the air or breath, which becomes sound or voice, can flow freely and easily in and out of you when you are speaking and singing.

You must always see that the muscles of your waist are drawn in gently and easily; that your chest, shoulders and neck are loose and free. All of the muscles of the upper part of your body must be so loose and free that nothing interferes with the flow of the air or breath.

All you do at first about breathing is to take a breath as often as you need one. As you continue to use all of your muscles correctly when you speak and sing, you will find that you can speak more words or sing longer phrases on one breath. You should never try to force yourself to speak or sing longer phrases than you have sufficient breath for as this will tense muscles that should be loose and free.

If you want to take a really deep breath, just for fun, feel as if the air were going out of the small of your back, opposite from where you have drawn in at your waist.

In my experience in helping speakers and singers, I have found that there is too much talk and concern about the diaphragm and breathing. I never do anything about either in my work in voice therapy and voice improvement. Cases of vocal disabilities are cured and speaking and singing voices improved without anything being done about the diaphragm or breathing.

You don't need to know anything at all about your

diaphragm in order to speak and sing properly. If you want to know what it looks like and how it functions, you can get all the information you wish from medical books. Trying to do something about it when speaking or singing can result in confusion and tensed muscles.

The same is true of the larynx and vocal cords. You don't need to know anything about them in order to speak and sing properly. As with the diaphragm, if you want to know what they look like and how they function, you can get all the information you wish from medical books.

From my experience in the usage of the muscles of the vocal instrument, it would seem that the flow of the air or breath is regulated by the muscles that produce the sounds. Since these muscles are not under your control, there is nothing you can do about regulating or controlling your breath other than to see that you are using all of the other muscles of your vocal instrument correctly. Trying to consciously control your breath when speaking and singing can result in confusion and tensed muscles.

Most of those who come to me for help with their voices are concerned about their breathing. Some have been told certain things they should do about it such as breathing from the diaphragm, breathing deeply or using various methods of breathing. Others have merely been told that they should do something about it.

This emphasis on breathing seems to be due to a lack of knowledge and understanding of the correct usage of the muscles of the upper part of the vocal instrument. It is the misusage of the muscles above the neck which makes a person feel as if there were something wrong with his breathing. It is not the fault of the breathing at all. When the student learns how to use all of the muscles of his vocal instrument correctly, what he thought were breathing difficulties go away without his doing anything about his breathing.

As you continue to use all of the muscles of your own vocal instrument correctly when you speak and sing, you will find that your air or breath will flow freely and easily in and out of you as it should. You won't have to do anything else about it.

Again, all you do at first is take a breath as often as you need one, in the middle of a word or phrase if necessary. Then, as you continue to use all of your muscles correctly, you will find that you can speak or sing longer phrases on each breath.

The exercise for the muscles of your waist is the last of the exercises which you use for keeping the muscles of your vocal instrument in good physical condition.

The exercises for the *AH* sounds you had in the previous lesson are the last of the exercises you use for saying sounds correctly.

This time practice reading in full voice without using the questions but feeling that your voice is filling up the room in the arch at the back of your mouth and floating freely and easily from your ears up. Feel as if you were talking to a large group of persons in a large auditorium.

When you are reading and speaking this way, always be sure that your cheeks are lifted gently and easily, that the hinges of your lower jaw are dropped loosely and freely and that your tongue is lying softly in your mouth, as if it were about to spill out over your lower front teeth.

When you speak loudly, as when addressing large groups of people or when speaking over noises, always feel that you are gently and easily making more room at the back of your mouth. Your voice will then carry over the noise or to the farthest corner of the room or auditorium without any effort on your part.

You must always have the feeling, especially when speaking in a large room or auditorium or when acting in the theatre, that every vowel sound you say, no matter how small, seemingly inconsequential or how rapidly spoken, fills up the entire room in the arch at the back of your mouth. Even a *the* or an *a* must fill this entire room.

The same is true when you are speaking softly or whispering. Every vowel sound must have its complete room in the arch at the back of the mouth.

Using this room inside your mouth is the last thing you learn to do. It is through the continued correct usage of this room that your voice continues to grow in volume, resonance and quality.

After you have practiced the exercises for the muscles at your waist, for saying the *AH* sounds and reading in full voice for a while; then make another recording of your voice. Read the same portion of the *Gettysburg Address* you read before you began your first lesson, without the questions and in full voice.

Play it back and then play back again the first two recordings you made. You will see how your own voice has grown in volume, resonance and quality.

Also, have another set of pictures taken of yourself saying See and Sah. Compare these with the pictures you had taken before your first lesson. You will see how your face has changed, how much more alive and interesting it has become.

As you continue to use or play on your vocal instrument correctly, your voice will continue to improve. There is really no limit to what you can do in improving your voice as you continue to use your vocal instrument correctly. You will find new things happening for you all the time.

The next chapter will tell you something about how to care for your vocal instrument as you continue to use it correctly.

Chapter Eleven

HOW TO CARE FOR YOUR
VOCAL INSTRUMENT

YOU HAVE NOW learned how to exercise and use correctly all of the muscles of your vocal instrument with which you are particularly concerned when speaking and singing; those of your cheeks, nose, lips, lower jaw, tongue, soft palate and waist.

You should continue to do all of the exercises you have been working on occasionally, just as you would go to a gymnasium to keep other muscles of your body in good physical condition.

Keeping all of the muscles of your vocal instrument in good physical condition means that you always have a good vocal instrument to play on when you speak and sing.

HOW TO PLACE YOUR INSTRUMENT

Before you begin to speak or sing, you must see that your vocal instrument is properly placed, just as the violinist places his violin on his shoulder or the cellist places his cello on its peg.

When placing your instrument, you first see that your feet are firmly planted on the floor, if standing, or that you are firmly seated on your chair, if sitting.

Then you draw in gently and easily at your waist and see that your chest, shoulders and neck are loose and free.

In other words, you see that your entire body, which is your entire vocal instrument, is in proper alignment.

HOW TO PREPARE YOUR INSTRUMENT

Just before you begin to speak or sing, you get ready just as the violinist does by placing his fingers over the strings and raising his bow, as the pianist does by placing his fingers over the keys.

Just before you begin to speak or sing, you prepare your vocal instrument by opening your mouth correctly and taking a breath.

When you open your mouth correctly your cheeks are lifted gently, your lower jaw is dropped loosely and freely and your tongue lies softly in your mouth, as if about to spill out over your lower front teeth. All of these things should now have become so automatic for you that they happen as one action as you take your breath.

You just open your mouth and take a breath.

HOW TO PLAY ON YOUR INSTRUMENT

Then you play on your instrument with vowel and consonant sounds.

You should see that you have made sufficient room, gently and easily, in the arch at the back of your mouth for your vowel sounds. They should float freely and easily into this room from your ears up, as if they were floating up back of your molars.

You see that your lips and tongue are soft, loose and free when you say the consonant sounds. You see that you spring quickly and easily from them to the vowel sounds that follow them. If the consonant sounds are not made freely and easily they interfere with the float of the vowel sounds.

Then you make your dramatic effects and shadings, your interpretations, as you feel them, just as any other instrumentalist does, with changes of pitch, tempo, volume, rhythm, etc.

You never change the shape of your instrument as you play on it any more than the violinist or pianist would change the shape of his violin or piano as he plays on it. The lips, tongue and lower jaw move about to shape the forms for the various vowel and consonant sounds but the shape and position of the vocal instrument remain the same. The body is always in proper alignment, the cheeks are always lifted and the complete room inside the mouth is always present.

You never sacrifice your vocal instrument to a language. The sounds produced when speaking or singing in any language must conform to the correct usage of the muscles of the vocal instrument.

I am often asked how you can smile and be serious when you're interpreting. You don't have to be smiling all of the time. We use the smile at first in order to feel the lift of the cheek muscles. However, the lift of the cheek muscles must be there no matter how serious or tragic the situation may be. The other muscles of your face then make your expressions for you. If the lift of your cheek muscles is not there, the expression on your face will be dull and uninteresting and the sounds of your voice will not carry.

Now that you have learned all about your vocal instrument and how to use it and play on it correctly, you can continue to improve your speaking voice by doing some singing.

Even if you have not sung before, or thought you could not sing or were tone deaf; you can have fun learning how to use your singing voice.

The next chapter will tell you more about it.

Chapter Twelve

SINGING

THE MUSCLES OF the vocal instrument are used in exactly the same way when singing as when speaking. The only difference is that the vowel sounds are sustained longer when singing.

Since it takes additional muscle strength to sustain the vowel sounds when singing, this additional strength you develop gives you additional muscle strength for your vowel sounds when speaking. There is nothing better for the speaking voice than singing, provided it is done correctly muscularly.

Conversely, the singer must always be using his muscles correctly when speaking if he expects his singing voice to improve. You cannot be using your muscles incorrectly all day when you are speaking and then expect them to function correctly when you are singing.

The next six chapters or lessons show you how to hum correctly, how to sing the different vowel sounds correctly and how to develop the additional muscle strength necessary for sustaining them on the higher tones.

Even though you do not intend to become a professional singer, you can have fun with the singing exercises and singing songs for your own pleasure and amusement.

It doesn't matter whether or not you have sung before. You can still have fun singing. I have had many students tell me they were tone deaf and could not sing. They really weren't tone deaf. It was just because they did not know how to use their muscles correctly that they could not sing. When they began to use them correctly when speaking, they found they could sing.

Before you begin the singing exercises, get a song book that has the song, "Drink To Me Only With Thine Eyes", in it. Most of the community song books include it. It is a beautiful old song and you will enjoy getting acquainted with it if you don't already know it. We will use it for all of our exercises.

If you are interested in singing popular music or show tunes, you can use "Oh, What a Beautiful Morning" from *Oklahoma* for practice.

Both of these songs lie in the middle range of the voice. This range is approximately from the E flat above middle C to the E flat an octave above for high voices and from middle C to the C an octave above for low voices.

This middle range is the foundation of your voice and you must first build correct muscle strength in this range through correct muscle usage. By using these songs for practice at first you can concentrate on what you are doing with your muscles, which is the important thing, without skipping around musically.

If you haven't a piano or other musical instrument from which to get your notes or pitches, get a chromatic pitch pipe. These are the ones that have all of the notes of the chromatic scale. You can get one at any music store. With this pitch pipe you can play any note or pitch on which to start a song. If you have not studied music, you can always get someone to tell you what note you should start on.

If you have a high voice, use the key of E flat. This is the key in which these songs usually come.

If you have a low voice, use the key of C.

If you are using a pitch pipe and have a high voice, begin on the G above middle C "Drink To Me Only" and on the B flat above middle C for "Oh, What a Beautiful Morning".

If you have a low voice, begin on the E above middle C for "Drink To Me Only" and on the G above middle C for "Oh, What a Beautiful Morning".

If you have not sung before, it is best to begin with the low key. As your muscles and voice grow stronger, you can go to higher keys. With some students I have had to start even lower than the key of C. I have even started in the key of A flat which means they begin on middle C for "Drink To Me Only" and the E flat above middle C for "Oh, What a Beautiful Morning". If you have any difficulty at all beginning on the pitch for the low voice, begin on a lower pitch where you feel comfortable. The important thing is to start where it is easy and comfortable for you. If you start too high you will strain the muscles of your throat.

You now know how to use all of the muscles of your vocal instrument correctly when you speak. All that you do now is to apply what you already know about them to singing. You should always approach your singing as you would approach your speaking. As we have already said, the only difference between speaking and singing is that the vowel sounds are sustained longer when singing.

The exercises that follow will help you gain the additional muscle strength you need for sustaining the vowel sounds.

Always use a mirror when you practice so that you can see that you are using your muscles correctly. The correct way to use them is shown in the pictures.

Chapter Thirteen

THE HUM

THE FIRST SOUND you will learn about is the hum.
Humming correctly is one of the best things you can do for both your speaking and singing voice. It is like giving your muscles a good massage. It is especially beneficial if you are suffering from a voice disorder which your physician says is due to your manner of speaking or singing.

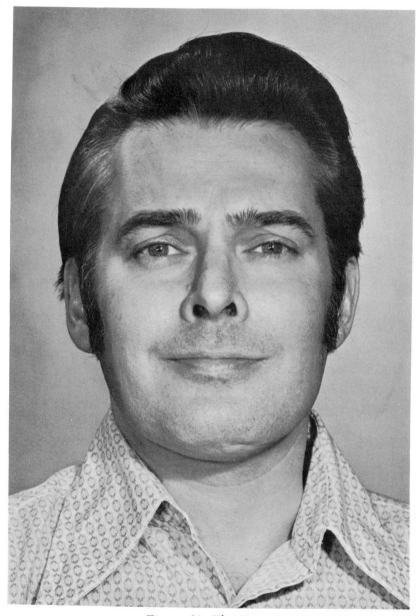

Figure 21. The Hum

When you hum correctly, you lift the muscles of your cheeks gently and have the sound of a soft *M* on your lips.

Hum the melody of the song you are using, "Drink To Me Only" or "Oh, What a Beautiful Morning", or just a phrase at first if you would rather, until you get used to humming.

Lift your cheeks gently, pout your lips softly and hum, with the sound of a soft *M* on your lips, as in Figure 21.

Let the sound of the hum float up freely and easily.

Take a breath as often as you need it.

As you continue to hum, feel that your head is loose and free on your neck, as if it could nod gently.

Figure 22. How to Test Your Hum

As you continue to hum, you can test for yourself whether or not you are humming correctly.

To do this, pluck your lower lip, as you would pluck a guitar string, with the index finger of your right hand while you are humming, as shown in Figure 22.

If you are humming correctly, you will get a sound like "mum-mum-mum-mum-mum."

If you have any difficulty getting the Mum sound when plucking, say the word Hum when you start and sustain the M sound. The Mum sound will then come through with the pluck. After you have felt the sensation of the Mum sound, it won't be necessary to say the word Hum in order to get it. You will be able to start right off with the soft M sound.

You must always have the sound of M on your lips when you hum. Never hum with an N or NG sound. If you will try humming with an *N* or *NG* sound, you will find that you can't get the Mum sound when you pluck.

After you have gotten the Mum sound with your pluck, continue to pluck your lips occasionally just to be sure that you are humming correctly.

Hum whenever you think of it, when you are walking around the house or on your way to work. Hum with your radio or TV, provided the music is within your range. Never try to force your voice to go higher or lower than it does easily and comfortably. If you do, you will strain your muscles instead of strengthening them.

As your muscles grow stronger and you can go higher, keep feeling that your hum is going farther back into the arch at the back of your mouth the higher you go. It should feel as if it were going out of the back of your head. Never try to make it come forward. This will tense your muscles and make it difficult for you to go higher. You should feel as if the arch at the back of your mouth were growing larger the higher you go. Be sure to keep the muscles of the hinges of your jaw loose and free as you go higher.

HOW TO BEGIN TO SING A SONG

You can try singing a song this time, too, whichever one

you have decided on, "Drink To Me Only" or "Oh What a Beautiful Morning."

All you do when you first begin to sing is to see that your cheeks are lifted gently and that the sounds of your voice are all floating up freely and easily, just as you have been doing when speaking.

So take your mirror, see that your cheeks are lifted gently all the time and sing the words. Don't let your cheeks drop unless it is between phrases and then be sure to see that they are lifted again before you begin the next phrase. That's all you do when you first begin to learn to sing correctly.

Concentrate on humming this time until the hum feels as if it were floating up freely and easily. Pluck your lips occasionally to see that you are humming correctly.

Also, be sure that your cheeks are lifted gently all the time when you are singing.

Chapter Fourteen

THE $\bar{E}$ SOUND

THIS TIME YOU will learn how to sing the sound of $\bar{E}$ as in See, correctly.

I have found that more people have trouble singing the sound of $\bar{E}$ than any other vowel sound. Most of the difficulty comes from trying to do something with the sound itself instead of trying to sing it correctly muscularly.

Some students have been taught to *place* the sound somewhere or to *sing it in the mask*, apparently meaning the upper front part of the face. You should never try to *place* sounds anywhere. Trying to *place* them somewhere can cause tense and constricted muscles and harsh and strident sounds. When you use all of your muscles correctly, the $\bar{E}$ sound is as easy to sing correctly as any other vowel sound.

Figure 23. $\overline{\text{E}}$

SEE

Sing the melody of the song you are using, singing See on each note.

Sing only a phrase or a note at first, if you wish. Then sing the entire melody with See after you have become familiar with singing the Ē sound.

Look in your mirror and see that your cheeks are lifted gently, as in Figure 23. Say the S sounds gently and easily. Then, as you sing, feel that the Ē sounds are floating up freely and easily.

As you continue to sing it, see that your tongue is lying softly in your mouth, as if about to spill out over your lower front teeth. It will then go where it should go when you sing the Ē sound.

Many people have a tendency to tense their tongues or pull them back into their mouths when singing the Ē sound. If you are doing this, you can see it pull back away from your lower front teeth. When the tendency of the muscles to pull back is very strong, you can see a space between the teeth and the front of the tongue. You cannot sing an Ē sound correctly if there is any tension in the muscles of your tongue.

As you continue to sing the Ē sound, see that your cheeks are lifted gently, that the hinges of your lower jaw are loose and free and that your tongue is lying softly in your mouth, as if about to spill out over your lower front teeth.

Your Ē sounds will then fill up the room in the arch at the back of your mouth in the same manner as all of your other vowel sounds should do.

Figure 24A.
Ē as in See

Figure 24B.
Ĭ as in Sit

Figure 24C.
Ĕ as in Set

Figure 24D.
Ă as in Sat

THE Ē GROUP OF VOWEL SOUNDS

The pictures on the opposite page show the group of vowel sounds we call the Ē group. These are the sounds of Ē as in See, Ĭ as in Sĭt, Ĕ as in Sĕt and Ă as in Săt.

You will notice that the opening of the mouth for the Ē sound is the smallest. Then the opening gets larger for each succeeding sound until it is largest for the Ă sound.

The room inside the mouth, in the arch at the back of the mouth, is also smallest for the Ē sound and gets larger for each succeeding sound until it is largest for the Ă sound.

However, no matter what the actual size of the room inside the mouth, we always try to feel as if it were as large as the room for the sound of AH, as in the exercise for the AH words, for all of these sounds.

Most people do not have any difficulty with the room at the back of the mouth on the Ĕ and Ă sounds. They naturally take more room than the Ē or Ĭ sounds. However, many do have difficulty at first when singing the Ē and Ĭ sounds.

If you do have any difficulty singing words with the Ē and Ĭ sounds in them, sing them as Ĕ at first. Then, after you have felt the room with the Ĕ sound, sing the Ē and Ĭ sounds using the same feeling of room inside your mouth that you had when singing the Ĕ sound.

In other words, when you sing "Drink To Me Only With Thine Eyes", sing words with the sound of Ē in them, such as Me and Leave, and words with the sound of Ĭ in them such as Drink and With, substituting Mĕ, Lĕve, Drĕnk and Wĕth until you have a feeling of room and freedom at the back of your mouth on the Ĕ sound. Then sing them correctly as Me, Leave, Drink and With using the same feeling of room and freedom in the arch at the back of your mouth as you had on the Ĕ sound.

As you sing higher tones with the Ē and Ĭ sounds, you must have the feeling of more opening at the front of your mouth and more and more room at the back of your mouth. On the higher tones your mouth should be as open and you should have as much room inside your mouth as when singing the sound of AH when you sing the Ē and Ĭ sounds.

When you sing them this way they will have the same quality as the rest of your vowel sounds and you will not sound, as do many singers, as if you had changed to another voice when you sing these sounds.

Sing your song with See this time. Continue to hum and to sing the song with your cheeks lifted gently and feeling that the sounds are floating up freely and easily.

Watch for words with $\bar{E}$ and $\breve{I}$ sounds in them. If you have any difficulty with them, try singing them as $\breve{E}$. You will find it will make them much easier for you to sing. When students have been in the habit of singing the $\bar{E}$ and $\breve{I}$ incorrectly, I sometimes find it necessary to have them sing them as $\breve{E}$ for quite a while until they overcome their old, incorrect habits.

Chapter Fifteen

THE $\overline{OO}$ SOUND

THIS TIME YOU will learn how to sing the sound of $\overline{OO}$, as in Moon, correctly.

This is another sound many people have difficulty with when singing. The difficulty is usually due to protruding or rounding the lips when singing it. This is, of course, incorrect usage of the lip muscles. The lips must never be rounded or protruded when singing any vowel sound. They must always be soft and free and away from the teeth. They must never cover the teeth.

When you use your muscles correctly when singing it, the $\overline{OO}$ sound is as easy to sing as any other vowel sound.

Figure 25. $\overline{OO}$

F$\overline{OO}$

This time sing the melody of your song with Foo, singing Foo on each note.

Sing only a phrase or a note at first, if you like. Then sing the entire melody with Foo after you have become familiar with singing the $\overline{OO}$ sound.

Look in your mirror and see that your cheeks are lifted gently, as in Figure 25. Say the F sounds gently and easily. As you sing, feel as if the $\overline{OO}$ sounds were floating up freely and easily.

Many people tense their tongues, particularly the backs of their tongues, when singing this sound. This constricts the muscles of the throat and makes it difficult to produce the sound.

As you continue to sing the $\overline{OO}$ sound, see that your cheeks are lifted gently, that the hinges of your lower jaw are loose and free and that your tongue is lying softly in your mouth, as if about to spill out over your lower teeth.

The $\overline{OO}$ sound will then fill up the room in the arch at the back of your mouth the same as all the other vowel sounds do.

Figure 26A.
O͞O as in Moon

Figure 26B.
O̅ as in Moan

Figure 26C.
AW as in Saw

Figure 26D.
AH as in Star

THE $\overline{OO}$ GROUP OF VOWEL SOUNDS

The pictures on the opposite page show the group of vowel sounds we call the $\overline{OO}$ group. These are the sounds of $\overline{OO}$ as in Moon, $\overline{O}$ as in Moan, *AW* as in Saw and *AH* as in Star.

You will notice, as with the $\overline{E}$ group, that the opening at the front of the mouth for the $\overline{OO}$ sound is the smallest. Then the opening gets larger for each succeeding sound until it is largest for the *AH* sound.

The room inside the mouth, in the arch at the back of the mouth, is also smallest for the $\overline{OO}$ sound and gets larger for each succeeding sound until it is largest for the *AH* sound.

However, no matter what the actual size of the room inside the mouth, we always try to feel as if it were as large as the room for the sound of *AH* for all of these sounds.

Most people do not have any difficulty with the room inside the mouth on the *AW* and *AH* sounds, as they naturally take more room. However, many do have difficulty at first when singing the $\overline{OO}$ and $\overline{O}$ sounds.

If you do have any difficulty with them, sing the $\overline{OO}$ and $\overline{O}$ sounds as *AW* at first. Then, after you have felt the room with the *AW* sound, sing the $\overline{OO}$ and $\overline{O}$ sounds using the same feeling of room inside your mouth that you had when singing the *AW* sound.

In other words, when you sing "Drink to Me Only With Thine Eyes", sing the words with the sound of $\overline{OO}$ in them, such as To, and with $\overline{O}$ in them, such as Only, substituting Taw and AWnly until you have a feeling of room and freedom at the back of your mouth on the *AW* sound. Then sing them correctly as To and Only using the same feeling of room and freedom in the arch at the back of your mouth as you had when singing the *AW* sound.

As you sing higher tones with the $\overline{OO}$ and $\overline{O}$ sounds, you must have the feeling of more opening at the front of your mouth and more and more room at the back of your mouth. On the higher tones your mouth should be as open and you should have as much room inside your mouth as when singing the sound of *AH* when you sing the $\overline{OO}$ and $\overline{O}$ sounds. When you sing them this way they will have the same quality as the rest of your vowel sounds.

Sing your song with Foo this time. Continue to hum it, to sing it with See and to sing the words with your cheeks lifted gently and feeling that the sounds are floating up freely and easily. It should be getting easy for you to do this now.

Watch for words with $\overline{OO}$ and $\overline{O}$ in them. If you have any difficulty with them, try singing them as *AW*. This will make it easy for you to sing them correctly. It is a good idea to practice singing these sounds this way for a while until you feel the room and freedom inside your mouth when singing them.

If you have some other songs you would like to try that lie in the middle range, E flat above middle C to the E flat an octave above for high voices, and middle C to the C an octave above for low voices, try singing them as you have been singing your song, with your cheeks lifted gently and feeling that all of the sounds are floating up freely and easily. Feel as if they were floating up freely and easily and out of your ears.

It is best to take songs at first that move along rhythmically. Don't make a lot of effort to sustain tones at first. As muscle strength comes in through singing freely and easily on this type of song, the vowel sounds will begin to sustain for a longer time by themselves without your trying to make them sustain.

If you try to sustain sounds longer than you are able to do freely and easily and as your muscle strength permits, you will tense the muscles you are trying to free and strengthen. Let the muscle strength necessary for sustaining the vowel sounds come in gradually of itself.

THE AW SOUNDS
—begins on next page

Chapter Sixteen

THE *AW* SOUND

I N THE LAST two lessons you learned how to sing the small vowel sounds, the sounds of $\bar{E}$ and $\overline{OO}$, correctly.

This time you will practice singing one of the larger vowel sounds, the sound of *AW*, as in Saw, which uses more room inside the mouth than the $\bar{E}$ or $\overline{OO}$ sounds.

However, you continue to use your muscles the same way you have been using them for the $\bar{E}$ and $\overline{OO}$ sounds. You lift your cheeks gently, drop the hinges of your lower jaw loosely and freely and let your tongue lie softly in your mouth, as if about to spill out over your lower teeth. The only difference is that you feel you have more room in the arch at the back of your mouth than you had on the $\bar{E}$ and $\overline{OO}$ sounds.

Figure 27. AW

VAW

This time sing Vaw on each note of the melody of your song.

Take your mirror and see that your cheeks are lifted gently, as in Figure 27.

Say the V sounds gently and easily.

Let the *AW* sounds float up freely and easily, as if up and out of your ears.

As you continue to practice, see that your lower jaw is dropped loosely and freely on its hinges. The muscles in front of your ears, which move the hinges, must feel soft and loose. You should feel as if the back of your lower jaw were dropping gently back under your ears. However, don't try to make it go back. It must drop of its own weight. There must be no tension in its hinges. It must feel as if it were dropping loosely and freely by itself, as if you had nothing to do with it.

Then see that your tongue is lying softly in your mouth, as if about to spill out over your lower teeth.

As you sing the *AW* sounds on higher notes, you must have the feeling that you are using more and more room in the arch at the back of your mouth until on the highest tones you feel as if you had as much room as you do when singing the *AH* sound, which requires the most room of all.

THE DIPHTHONGS

This time you will also learn about a group of vowel sounds we call diphthongs. Diphthongs are combinations of vowel sounds.

There are five of these combinations of sounds as follows:

$\overline{I}$ as in Night,	a combination of *AH* and $\overline{E}$
OU as in Round,	a combination of *AH* and $\overline{OO}$
OI as in Boil,	a combination of *AW* and $\breve{I}$
AY as in Say,	a combination of $\breve{E}$ and $\overline{\overline{E}}$
$\overline{U}$ as in Fume,	a combination of $\overline{E}$ and $\overline{OO}$

In the first four diphthongs, the first vowel sound of the combination is sustained the longer.

In the last, the second vowel sound is sustained the longer.

When you sing these diphthongs properly, you should always sing each combination as if it consisted of only the longer of the two vowel sounds, just touching the other vowel sound lightly and quickly.

Always sing them as follows:

$\overline{I}$ as *AH*,   night as nAHēt
OU as *AH*,   round as rAH$\overline{oo}$nd
OI as *ĂW*,   boil as b̧AW̆il
AY as *Ĕ*,   say as sĔē̄
$\overline{U}$ as $\overline{OO}$,   fume as fē$\overline{OO}$m

Watch for any of these diphthongs as you sing "Drink To Me Only With Thine Eyes", "Oh, What a Beautiful Morning" and any other songs you are singing; and practice singing them this way.

Sing Thine as ThAHēn, touching the $\overline{E}$ lightly just before the *N*. Never hold the $\overline{E}$ part of the sound. Sing Thou as ThAH$\overline{oo}$, touching the $\overline{OO}$ part lightly as you finish. Don't sustain the $\overline{OO}$ part. Watch out particularly for the *AY* sound. Many singers go immediately to the $\overline{E}$ part of the combination, making a word such as Say sound as if they were singing See. The Ĕ part of the combination should be sustained and the $\overline{E}$ part just touched lightly.

Sing your song with Vaw this time. Be sure to look in your mirror to see that you are using your cheeks, lower jaw and tongue correctly. Continue humming and singing your song with See, Foo and the words, always watching in your mirror to see that you are using your muscles correctly as shown in the pictures and as described in the exercises.

If you have some songs you would like to sing that go a little higher in pitch, try them this time. However, don't at this time go higher than an F if you have a high voice or a D if you have a low voice. It is best to go to higher tones gradually as you feel more muscle strength come in. As the higher tones you are singing become easy for you to sing, you can go on to still higher ones. If you try to sing tones that are higher than you are ready for muscularly, you may strain the muscles of your throat.

Chapter Seventeen

THE *AH* SOUND

N OW THAT YOU have learned how to use more room inside
your mouth by singing the *AW* sound correctly, this time
you will practice singing the sound of *AH*, as in Star, which
physically requires the most room inside the mouth.

You use your muscles the same way when you sing the
AH sound as you have been using them when singing the
other vowel sounds. You lift your cheeks gently, drop the
hinges of your lower jaw loosely and freely and let your tongue
lie softly in your mouth, as if about to spill out over your
lower front teeth.

The only difference is that you feel as if you had gently
and easily made more room at the back of your mouth for
the *AH* sound to float into. This you do by feeling that your
lower jaw is drooping farther on its hinges, loosely and
freely, almost as if it were drooping back under your ears.
When you open your mouth correctly this way, you are
prepared and ready to sing the *AH* sound.

You cannot do anything about the structure of your upper
jaw when making more room inside your mouth for resonating
your vowel sounds. You get the feeling of more room by
dropping the hinges of your lower jaw loosely and freely. It
is as if your lower molars were hanging loosely separated
from your upper ones. Don't try to force it lower. Just let
it hang there of its own weight.

Figure 28. AH

LAH

This time sing Lah on each note of the melody of your song.

Take your mirror and see that your cheeks are lifted gently, as in Figure 28.

Let your tongue wave gently and easily when you say the L sounds.

Let the *AH* sounds float up freely and easily, as if up and out of your ears.

As you continue to practice, see that your lower jaw is dropped loosely and freely on its hinges, as if it were dropping gently back under your ears, and that your tongue is lying softly in your mouth, as if about to spill out over your lower teeth.

As you sing the *AH* sounds on higher notes, you must feel that you are gently and easily making more and more room in the arch at the back of your mouth.

The *AH* sound requires the most room inside your mouth. However, you should feel as if you had the same amount of room when singing all of the vowel sounds, even the $\bar{E}$ and $\overline{OO}$ sounds, which actually take the least amount of room. You should feel as if every vowel sound were filling the entire room in the arch at the back of your mouth. You should always feel as if you had the room for the *AH* sound back of every vowel sound you sing, as if you had that same amount of room for each vowel sound.

You should feel as if your mouth were opening at the back instead of the front. The front of your mouth becomes very unimportant as you continue to use the room at the back of your mouth correctly. Opening the front of the mouth too wide, or forcing it open, can close in on the room at the back.

THE $\breve{U}$, $\breve{OO}$ AND *ER* SOUNDS

When you sing the sounds of $\breve{U}$ as in Cup, $\breve{OO}$ as in Book and *ER* as in Her, you should also have the feeling that you are using the room of the *AH* sound. This applies also to the *IR* sound as in Fir and the *UR* sound as in Urgent.

When you sing your songs, sing such words as Cup, Would and Thirst in "Drink To Me Only With Thine Eyes" this way, with the feeling that you are singing each *U, OO* and *ER, IR* or *UR* sound as *AH*.

Sing them as cAHp, wAHd and thAHrst at first until you have a feeling of room and freedom inside your mouth. Then sing them as Cup, Would and Thirst with the feeling of the same room and freedom you had when singing them with *AH*. In this way you keep them as open as the other vowel sounds and they will not close in on the room inside your mouth and make it difficult for you to sing them.

For this time sing your practice song, and any of the other songs you are studying in the middle range, with Lah on each note. Look in your mirror to see that you are using your muscles correctly.

Continue to hum and to sing your song with See, Foo, Vaw and the words.

As you keep on practicing songs you are studying, watch in your mirror to see that your cheeks are lifted gently, that your lower jaw is dropped loosely and freely and that your tongue is lying softly in your mouth, as if about to spill out over your lower teeth.

These are the three most important things to watch for in your mirror as you continue with your singing.

Now that you have finished this chapter, you know what to do with all of your vowel sounds. What you do now is to apply what you already know as you continue to sing songs and to build your singing voice.

The next chapter will give you some advice on what to do as you build it.

HOW TO BUILD YOUR
SINGING VOICE
—begins on next page

Chapter Eighteen

HOW TO BUILD YOUR
SINGING VOICE

Y OU NOW KNOW how to exercise all of the muscles of your vocal
instrument correctly so that you can keep them in good physical condition.

You also know how to use them correctly when you say
all of the vowel and consonant sounds and you know how
to build the additional muscle strength you need for sustaining
the vowel sounds when you sing.

The kind of singing voice you have depends on the physical
condition of the muscles of your vocal instrument and the
way you use them when you speak and sing. By keeping
them in good physical condition and using them correctly
when you speak and sing, you can have the best voice possible
from the vocal instrument nature has given you.

As you continue to build your singing voice, you must first
see that you build muscle strength for your middle voice
through correct muscle usage. This is the most important part
of your voice. It is the foundation for your voice. You cannot
sing higher or lower tones correctly unless you are first singing
correctly in your middle range.

As we have said before, in high female voices the middle
range lies approximately from the E flat above middle C to
the E flat an octave above. In low female voices it lies approximately from middle C to the C an octave above. The ranges
for male voices lie an octave below the female ranges.

You have become familiar with the middle range by singing
"Drink To Me Only With Thine Eyes" and "Oh, What a

Beautiful Morning." You should first study and sing songs that lie approximately within this range. There are many collections of songs in English and other languages, particularly in Italian, that lie within this range. There is nothing better for this purpose than singing some of the old Italian songs. For those of you who are interested in popular songs and show tunes, there are many of these which also lie within this range.

There are many books of vocal exercises which you can use to help yourself in building your higher tones, once you have become familiar with singing correctly in the middle part of your voice. However, it is of no use to practice vocal exercises without first knowing how to use your muscles correctly when practicing them. Use only exercises that begin with consonant sounds. Do not practice exercises that use only vowel sounds, that is, where the vowel sounds are not preceded by consonant sounds.

When singing in your middle range feels comfortable and easy, then choose songs or exercises that use notes a half tone higher than the highest note of the middle range. When singing these tones feels comfortable and easy, then choose other songs and exercises that go another half tone higher. Continue to go higher in this way, as muscle strength comes in and your singing feels comfortable and easy. You must approach the singing of your high tones gradually, preferably a half tone at a time. If you try to sing high tones before you are ready for them muscularly, you can place a strain on the muscles of your throat and vocal cords.

The high tones come in gradually as muscle strength comes in through correct muscle usage when producing them. They are produced muscularly in the same manner as the middle tones. All you do as you go higher is to feel that you are gently and easily making more and more room in the arch at the back of your mouth. As you make this room, you see that your cheeks are lifted gently, that the hinges of your lower jaw are dropped loosely and freely and that your tongue is lying softly in your mouth, as if about to spill out over your lower teeth.

The vowel sounds, which are your tones, float up into this

room which you have made, gently and easily, at the back of your mouth, behind your molars. The feeling should be that your vowel sounds are floating up freely and easily behind them, as if out of your ears, out of the back of your head. Your lower jaw and tongue are then hanging loosely and freely in front of your tones or vowel sounds and do nothing to interfere with them.

As you go higher in pitch, you should feel that your vowel sounds are going farther back into the room inside your mouth. You should feel as if the arch at the back of your mouth were enlarging backward and upward, as if it were as large as the stage you are on or the room you are in. You should feel that your vowel sounds are floating from your ears up, as if they were floating up and out of the back of your head. Any feeling of trying to bring the tones or vowel sounds forward can cause tension and strain in your muscles and close in on the room inside your mouth.

The low tones also come in gradually. They are produced muscularly in the same manner as the middle tones. You must have the same feeling of room at the back of your mouth when singing the low tones as you have when singing the middle and high tones.

When singing all tones, which are the vowel sounds (even the smallest, the $\bar{E}$ and $\overline{OO}$ sounds), you must have the feeling of room at the back of your mouth. They all float up into the room in the arch at the back of your mouth. As you continue to build your singing voice you must always have the feeling, whether you are singing words on the same pitch or whether you are going higher or lower, that you are constantly making more and more room and freedom at the back of your mouth.

Difficulty when singing a certain vowel sound on a high tone is often due to not having sufficient room inside the mouth on the vowel sound preceding the vowel sound on the high tone. When there is not sufficient room on a vowel sound preceding a high tone, the muscles are not able to move fast enough to make the room necessary for the high tone. Always be sure that you feel the same amount of room in the arch at the back of your mouth on a vowel sound preceding a high tone that you will need for the high tone.

The important thing to remember as you build your singing voice is that your voice is merely the result of the way in which you use the muscles of your vocal instrument when you sing.

For keeping each set of muscles in good physical condition, you should continue to practice the simple exercises for your cheeks, nose, lips, lower jaw, tongue, soft palate and waist.

You should keep up the exercises for all of the consonant sounds, the S Sounds, the miscellaneous consonant sounds, the Lip Sounds and the Tongue Sounds so that you are always using your muscles correctly when you say them. You should always see that you spring quickly and easily from all of the consonant sounds. Consonant sounds that are not said correctly muscularly interfere with the production and float of the vowel sounds that follow them.

You should also keep up the exercises using the Hum, See, Foo, Vaw and Lah so that you remind yourself of how you should be singing your vowel sounds.

Then read over and over and always keep in mind the instructions for playing on your vocal instrument correctly; for placing it, preparing it and playing on it properly.

The final thing to do when playing on it properly is to see that you spring quickly and easily from your consonant sounds and that you have sufficient room in the arch at the back of your mouth for your vowel sounds. They should all feel as if they were floating up back of your molars, up and out of your ears, out of the back of your head.

The better the physical condition of your vocal instrument and the better you play on it, the better your singing voice will be.

When your vocal instrument is in the best possible physical condition and you play on it correctly muscularly, your voice will be of the best quality that your own particular vocal instrument is capable of producing.

Chapter Nineteen

SOME STUDENTS AND
THEIR PROBLEMS

I THOUGHT THAT perhaps telling about some of my former students and their problems with certain muscles of their vocal instruments might be of interest and help to you with your own vocal problems. Your own problems might be similar to those of some of these students who overcame their vocal difficulties through the use of the material given in this book.

THE CHEEKS

A young actor who came to me because of his stammer could hardly move the muscles of his cheeks at all. He had been acting in the theatre for many years but had begun to stammer several years before. The stammering gradually increased until it became so bad he had to give up his profession. When he came to me it was difficult for him to carry on an ordinary conversation. He had sung as a boy soprano but when his voice changed he had such difficulty singing that his teacher told him he would never be able to sing again.

It was almost impossible for him to move the muscles of the upper part of his face at all when he began. He would close his eyes, concentrate on the muscles of his cheeks and then try to move them. He got only a few muscle twitches at first but gradually more and more muscle movement came in and eventually he was able to move them about freely and easily.

After learning to use these muscles correctly and then to

relieve the tension in the muscles of his lips, tongue and lower jaw, he was able to speak to people again. He then studied radio announcing and passed his interviews for work in that field. Then he decided he wanted to sing again. When he first began it sounded as if his former teacher were right. There were no singing tones in his voice. However, after several years of study and through sheer determination on his part, he passed his auditions and sang in the chorus of one of our leading opera companies. His voice continued to improve to where he was able to sing the title role in Gianni Schicchi.

Another young man was referred to me by his physician because of an ache he felt in his throat when speaking. His physician felt his manner of speaking was causing the ache. His throat bothered him so much at his job of selling that he thought he was going to have to give up his work. He soon found that the exercises for saying words with his cheeks lifted and as if asking questions gave him a feeling for the correct muscle level of his voice. It did not feel as if it were dropping onto his throat but floated up into his head. When speaking this way his throat did not ache. From then on, whenever he felt the ache coming on during the day and he knew he was going back to his old habits, he would go to another room and say "See Me Please" with the questions a few times. This gave him the feeling of how he should be speaking and he would go on selling without any difficulty for a while. Eventually the correct muscle usage became habit and he no longer had to remind himself of it.

A young man who used his voice a great deal on the telephone in his work was sent to me by his physician because of trouble he was having with his throat. After speaking all day at work, his throat hurt so badly he would stop talking when he arrived home and wrap it in hot, damp towels. When he came to me for the first few times he said he still felt some soreness at the end of the day. He felt the soreness as he was telling me about it. He was speaking a little below his natural muscle level and dropping onto the muscles of his throat. The drop onto his throat was not as bad as it had been but there was just enough to cause an irritation that made his throat sore.

As we worked together with the lift of his cheek muscles and saying words as if asking questions his voice would get onto its proper level again. The soreness would go away as we were talking and reading and he would leave without any feeling of soreness at all. The correct muscle habits had not been sufficiently established as yet. When talking all day he would drop back into his old habits at times. He would speak on too low a muscle level and the muscles of his throat and vocal cords would become irritated. By the time he had completed his study, he no longer had to use the hot towels. In fact, his new voice felt so good he decided to study acting.

Another student, when he came back for his second lesson, told me about the favorable reactions he had noticed since his first lesson. He had always had difficulty in making himself heard when speaking to groups of people in a large room. He would see them leaning forward in their chairs, straining to hear what had to say. This upset him and made it even more difficult for him to speak. This week he had to give another talk in the same large room. He felt very much pleased with what he had done with his voice in a week's time. He had gotten the idea of letting his voice float up as he was using the lift of his cheek muscles. He said he knew his voice was carrying out to his audience as they were all sitting comfortably and relaxed in their chairs. No one was straining to hear what he had to say.

Students whose work entails waiting on the public have an excellent opportunity for using their cheek muscles and asking questions. They can say, with a smile, "Good morning. May I help you?", "May I show you something else?", "Would you be interested in this?" This reminds them during the day of how they should be using their voices.

A young lady who wanted to improve her voice for use at her office told me she could not say "straight across the street" correctly. She was saying "shtraight acrosh zhe shtreet". She was speaking with collapsed facial muscles. Her tongue was lying at the bottom of her mouth and the air was going out along her lower jaw. When she learned to use her cheek muscles correctly, her tongue could go where it was supposed to go and the air could go where it was supposed to go and she had no trouble saying "straight across the street".

Another young lady could not do the work she wanted to do in the theatre because of her lisp. When she learned how to use her facial muscles correctly her lisp disappeared.

THE NOSE

A young man, a teacher, came to me whose nasal muscles were so tensed and pulled down that he was unable to move them at all. He could not advance in his profession because of the peculiar quality of his voice which resulted from misusing his facial muscles. When he spoke he pulled the muscles of his lips to one side and the muscles of his nose along with them until it looked as if he were speaking out of a small hole in the side of his face. He thought he had acquired the habit as a boy by trying to imitate a choir singer who sang with his mouth turned to one side. Later on the habit became so fixed in his own speech that he was unable to do anything about it.

The first thing I asked him to do was to try to lift the muscles of his cheeks as we do in the cheek exercise. When I saw he could not do this, I asked him to try to wrinkle up the bridge of his nose as we do in our exercise for the nose. I thought this might be easier for him to do and showed him how to do it. I was looking at him across the piano and saw no muscle movement at all. I thought he had not understood me so I said, "Won't you just try to move the muscles of your nose, like this?" There was still no movement of these muscles. I thought he might be a little embarrassed at making faces, as some people are at first, so I said to him again, "Won't you just try to move them?"

I had gotten up from the piano bench just as he was saying through clenched teeth, "I am trying". Standing in front of him I could see that his hands were clenched and his whole body rigid from the tremendous effort he was putting forth in trying to move the muscles of his nose. However, by patiently trying, he was soon able to move them. As he continued to practice all of the muscle exercises, the muscles of his face resumed their normal positions when speaking and he was able to help himself out of his vocal difficulties.

An attorney who had almost lost his voice was sent to me by his physician. He had developed a habit of pulling the muscles of the lower part of his nose down in order to try to force his voice out. The louder he tried to talk, the harder he pulled them down. When people are in vocal difficulties and don't know what to do to help themselves, they develop all sorts of odd muscle habits in trying to get their voices out. When pulling down the muscles of his nose, he also pulled down the muscles of his neck until he wore a shirt collar two sizes larger than he should have. After learning how to use his muscles correctly, he was able to speak in court easily, the nasal quality left his voice, and his neck returned to its normal size.

THE LIPS

A woman who had a small node on one of her vocal cords was sent to me by her physician. Nodes are corn-like growths on the vocal cords that result from a strain on the muscles due to improper muscle usage when speaking or singing. She had the usual raspy voice that results from the growths.

As she was telling me of her difficulties, I noticed that she was holding her upper lip tightly over her teeth as she spoke. I told her this was what was causing the strain on her throat and vocal cords that had resulted in the node. After bringing this to her attention, she said that as a girl she had worn bands on her teeth and had tried to hide them by holding her upper lip over them. The bands had long since been removed but the habit of holding her lip over her teeth had remained.

After she learned how to use her muscles correctly, the node went away, the rasp left her voice and she was able to sing again; something she had not been able to do for many years.

A young lady came to me who had had a node removed from one or her vocal cords. Her throat was still bothering her when she spoke. She worked in an office and talked to people and used the telephone a great deal each day. When nodes that result from incorrect muscle usage when speaking or singing are removed and the muscle behavior is not changed, they quite frequently come back again. The strain that caused them originally still continues.

As she was telling me of her trouble, I noticed that she was holding the left side of her upper lip over her teeth. I told her this pulled down lip was causing the strain on her throat and vocal cords and showed her how to lift it away correctly by using her cheek muscles. She said, "Oh, I can't do that. The lower part of this tooth is broken off and I don't want to show it". I told her it would be cheaper for her to have the tooth taken care of properly than to have another operation on her vocal cords, which would no doubt have been necessary had she continued speaking with the pulled down lip. She was not anxious to have another operation so she had the tooth fixed. She then learned how to use her muscles correctly and eventually had no further trouble with her throat or voice.

THE LOWER JAW

An attorney who was having trouble with his throat was sent to me by his physician. He said his voice was so bad he could not make himself understood in a court room. He was afraid he would not be able to continue in his profession. I noticed he was holding his jaws very close together when he was telling me of his troubles. He hardly opened his mouth. When I told him it was his tense jaw muscles that were causing most of his trouble, he said his dentist had told him he was always afraid he would crack his teeth when he closed his mouth, the muscles of his jaws were so powerful. When he learned to use them correctly, along with his other muscles, his throat no longer bothered him and he was able to be heard in court.

A woman who talked to groups of people all day in her work was referred to me by her physician. Her throat ached constantly when she was speaking. Her trouble, too, was due to speaking with tense and constricted jaw muscles. When I mentioned this to her she said her husband told her she ground her teeth at night. A woman in her office also told her she noticed her grinding her teeth when sitting at her desk. The tension in her jaw muscles had caused a terrific tension in the back of her neck and was the cause of the ache in her throat. When she learned how to use her muscles correctly, the tension in the back of her neck and the ache in her throat went away and she was able to talk all day long at her work without any difficulty.

THE TONGUE

A singer came to me who complained about what she called a "hole in her voice". In the lower part of her singing voice she was never sure what kind of sounds, if any, were going to come out. I asked her to sing for me. As she sang, I noticed the muscles of her tongue were tensed and pulled back from her lower teeth. I mentioned this to her. She said she had always felt as if there were a string on each side of her tongue pulling it back. She had mentioned this to other teachers but had been told to forget about it. Forgetting about it was not the answer. She had to learn what to do about it. After learning how to use her muscles correctly, the "hole" in her voice disappeared and she was able to sing the tones easily and without fear.

I am often asked by students what my tongue is doing when I show them how to say or sing certain sounds. I always have to tell them that I don't know. I have to look in a mirror to find out. I really don't feel my tongue at all excepting when it makes the Tongue Sounds and only on these sounds when

I stop to think about it. When you are using all of the muscles of your vocal instrument correctly and you have learned to leave your tongue lying softly in your mouth, it does what it should be doing without your being conscious of it.

THE SOFT PALATE

A woman was sent to me by her physician who said the hoarseness she was troubled with was due to a thickening of her vocal cords. The hoarseness was so bad that she was hardly able to speak at the end of the day.

Her trouble was mainly due to the collapsed muscles of her soft palate. When we came to the exercise for strengthening it, it was impossible for her to move it at all. It was the most difficult of all the exercises for her.

She said she had been told her voice was too high and she had tried to lower it. Trying to lower the pitch of her voice without knowing what she was doing with her muscles had caused her soft palate to sag. This caused the strain on the muscles of her throat that had resulted in the thickened cords and hoarseness. She was eventually able to move her soft palate easily. After learning to use all of her muscles correctly, the thickened vocal cords returned to normal, the hoarseness went away; and she was able to speak at her work all day without any difficulty.

You should never try to change the pitch of your voice, to try to make it higher or lower. When you use all of your muscles correctly, your voice will be on its own natural pitch. Trying to raise or lower the pitch of your voice without knowing what you are doing with your muscles can result in a strain on the muscles of your throat and vocal cords.

A young woman was sent to me because of almost complete loss of voice after a thyroidectomy. She could only speak in a weak whisper. In her case, too, the muscles of her soft palate were collapsed. It was impossible for her to move them at first. However, she was eventually able to move the muscles of her soft palate easily. When she learned how to use them correctly, along with the other muscles she used when speaking, her voice returned to normal.

PROJECTION

A clergyman was sent to me by his physician because of his weak, ineffective voice. His physician said his vocal cords did not come together properly when he spoke. He could not be heard when preaching a sermon and those who came to him for help thought he was not interested in their problems. When he had finished his work with me, he did all of the Lenten services for one of the larger churches in his city. I went to hear him and sat in the last row of pews. His voice filled the church and I could hear every word.

One day some time later he came to me and said, "I don't know what was the matter last Sunday. A member of the congregation came to me and asked if I were not feeling well. I felt that my voice was not carrying through as it had been doing". I asked him what he had been trying to do. He said, "I was trying to make my voice go back to the farthest end of the church". I said, smiling, "Oh, you were, were you?" He had been trying to project his voice and had tensed his muscles instead of just opening up the room at the back of his mouth and letting the sounds of his voice fill it. As I said this, he remembered what we had said before and said contritely, "Oh, I forgot". He had no more trouble with projection.

ALIGNMENT OR POSTURE

A woman who read to groups of people was sent to me because of some trouble she was having with her voice. She said she felt a constant strain on her throat and had difficulty in getting her voice out. She also complained about always being out of breath.

I asked her to read for me. As she read, I noticed that her body was tilted forward from her waist and her chin was pointed as if she were reading to the ceiling. I told her it was her posture that was causing her vocal difficulties and showed her how the way she was standing and holding her head was causing the strain on her throat. When she learned about her muscles and how to keep her body in proper alignment, the strain on her throat went away, her voice came through easily and she no longer felt short of breath.

BREATHING

A young lady, a teacher, was sent to me by her physician because of strain and fatigue she was feeling when teaching classes all day. After she had learned to use her muscles correctly and was speaking correctly, I was having her give me a lecture in full voice such as she would use in her classroom. After speaking for some time, she suddenly stopped, crossed her hands over her chest and screamed, "I'm not breathing!" I laughed and told her she must be as she was still standing up. She then laughed, too, but said she was really frightened for a moment. It had always been such an effort for her to breathe when she was speaking incorrectly in her classrooms. Now, when she did not feel anything going on, she said she really thought she must have stopped breathing. This all came about of itself without any mention of breathing but by seeing that all of the muscles she used in speaking were being used correctly.

SINGING

The vocal difficulties of many of the singers who have come to me for help have been due to their having been taught to produce tones or sounds in a manner contrary to the correct usage of the muscles of the vocal instrument. In some cases these misusages had resulted in loss of the singing voice.

Some had been told to protrude and round their lips when singing the $\overline{OO}$ and $\overline{O}$ sounds. This is, of course, contrary to correct usage of the lip muscles. The muscles of the cheeks must be lifted on all vowel sounds and this protrusion of the lips pulls the cheek muscles down and closes in on the room inside the mouth.

Others had been taught to do things with their tongues such as lowering the back of the tongue, making grooves in the tongue and making positions for it for various vowel and consonant sounds. Trying to make the tongue, especially the back of the tongue, do something can tense and constrict the tongue muscles. The tongue must always lie softly in its groove of saliva. The only thing we ask it to do is to wave gently up and down when we say the tongue consonants. This waving of the front of the tongue becomes so automatic that we are not conscious of it.

Still others had been told to lower the larynx. This is one of the worst things you can do to your vocal instrument. The muscles of the larynx and vocal cords must be left absolutely alone so that they are free to function normally. This they can do when all of the other muscles of the vocal instrument are used correctly. You must never attempt to control the muscles of your larynx or vocal cords when speaking or singing.

Many phrases are used with reference to singing which are confusing to the student. These phrases have to do with the sounds that are produced, the voice or tones, which are the effect, and not with the muscles of the vocal instrument that produce them, which are the cause.

Tone placement, voice placement and *singing in the mask* are typical examples. When you are using the muscles of your vocal instrument correctly the vibrating air or breath floats up into the room at the back of your mouth, which is where it should go. You don't *place* the air or sounds, which are vibrating air, anywhere. Trying to *place* them somewhere can result in tense and constricted muscles and a closing in on the room inside the mouth which is necessary for resonating all vowel sounds, which are your tones.

Singing on a line or in *bel canto* style can also be confusing since it is not always clear just what is meant by these terms. Presumably what is meant by these phrases is that the vowel sounds are all sustained correctly so that one flows into the next. If you are using the room in the arch at the back of your mouth correctly, this happens for you without your doing anything about it other than seeing that each vowel sound you sing is filling up the room in the arch at the back of your mouth.

Projection and *breath control* are two other confusing and often harmful terms. When you use your vocal instrument correctly, it *projects* the sounds of your voice for you. You cannot *project* sounds yourself. Trying to *project* your voice can result in tense and constricted muscles.

Breath control and the various types of breathing that go with it are always confusing to the student. You should never try to *control* your breath. When you use your entire vocal instrument, which is your entire body, correctly, the air or breath flows in and out of you freely and easily as it should. You have nothing to do with *controlling* it.

When you try to do something about your diaphragm or breathing, such as speaking or singing from your diaphragm, you are going in the wrong direction. You should be thinking about what you are doing with the upper part of your vocal instrument, the part from your neck up. Your diaphragm will then take care of itself. You have nothing to do about it.

A student whose vocal difficulties had worsened when he was told he should *sing from his diaphragm,* suddenly exclaimed, "Oh, I've been cut loose from my diaphragm", when he had achieved the correct usage of the upper part of his vocal instrument and his voice was responding correctly.

Another student, who had been taught similarly with reference to her diaphragm, exclaimed, "I've been cut loose from my stomach", when she also had achieved the correct usage of the upper part of her vocal instrument. Concentrating on her diaphragm had tensed and constricted muscles which felt to her as if they were her stomach muscles.

Some had been taught to throw their voices to the corner of the room or to the ceiling. The concentration is always on the voice, which is the result, and not on the usage of the vocal instrument, which is the cause.

The terms *register, head register* or *head voice, chest register* or *chest voice* are often very confusing. By these terms I presume is meant the division of the voice into various sections according to certain changes or adjustments of the muscles of the vocal instrument in producing sounds that seem to occur more obviously when singing at certain pitches.

Changes and adjustments occur to a lesser degree, of course, at all pitches.

When you are using the muscles of your vocal instrument correctly you are not concerned with *registers*. Whatever changes or adjustments in muscle usage that are necessary take place for you automatically as you use the muscles of your vocal instrument correctly. You don't try to do anything about them. You just see that you have made, easily and gently, sufficient room in the arch at the back of your mouth as these changes or adjustments take place for you. All tones, whether low, middle or high are produced in the same manner muscularly.

The use of the phrase *covered tone* is also confusing. I presume that what is meant is the tone floating into the correctly used arch at the back of the mouth, back of your molars.

In order to get this so-called *covered tone*, many students have been taught to pull down the backs of their tongues or to lower the larynx, which causes tense and constricted muscles and vocal difficulties on the higher tones. I have even seen tongue depressors used on the back of the tongue to try to achieved a *covered tone*.

All tones are produced in the same manner when you are using the muscles of your vocal instrument correctly. You do not have a different manner of producing them for different pitches. As you go to the higher tones or pitches you have the feeling that you are always making, gently and easily, more room in the arch at the back of your mouth. You do not change your manner of producing them muscularly.

There are many *methods* of *voice production* taught which are no doubt well understood by those who teach them but which are often confusing to the student. One student told me she had been told she must be able to inhale and exhale at the same time in order to sing properly. She had never been able to accomplish this and I doubt that I would be able to do so either.

Always remember, no matter what method of voice production you may look into, never to do anything that is contrary to the correct usage of the muscles of your vocal instrument.

APPENDIX

Diacritical Markings Used

Ă   as in Sat
Ē   as in See
Ĕ   as in Set
Ĭ   as in Sit
Ī   as in Night
Ō   as in Moan
OO as in Moon
ŎŎ as in Book
Ŭ   as in Cup

INDEX

A

Alignment, xii, 67, 69, 70, 74, 76, 122, 123
Arch, soft palate, 55, 57, 59, 63, 65, 67, 72, 75, 85, 89, 91, 95, 97, 101, 103, 107, 111, 112, 113, 124, 126
Articulation, 5

B

Bel canto style, 124
Bone structure, 11
Breath control, 125
Breathing, xii, 70–72, 75, 83, 122, 123, 125, 126

C

Cavity,
  head, 11
  oral, 25
Cheeks, xi, xii, 3, 19, 20, 25, 33, 41, 53, 59, 63, 64, 67, 72, 74, 76, 86, 89, 92, 95, 98, 101, 103–105, 107, 108, 111
Cheek muscles, 3, 4, 10–17, 20, 25, 29, 31, 35, 40, 41, 45, 47, 51, 55, 57, 74, 76, 83, 114–117, 119, 123
Cheek muscle exercise, 10–16, 20, 23, 24, 33, 40, 113, 115, 117
Chest, 74
Chest muscles, 69, 70
Chest register, 125
Chest voice, 125
Chromatic pitch pipe, 78
Chromatic scale, 78
Consonant Sounds, xi, 25, 35, 40, 41, 43, 53, 75, 110, 111, 113, 124
Contact ulcer, 4
Covered tone, 126
Curtis, H.H., vii, viii

D

Deaf adult, 5
Deaf child, 5
Deafness, tone, 76, 77
Diacritical markings, 127
Diaphragm, 70, 71, 125
Diphthongs, xii, 103, 104

E

Elkus, M.M., vii, viii
Exercises,
  cheek muscle, 10–16, 20, 23, 24, 33, 40, 113, 115, 117
  lapping, 46, 47, 55
  licking, 44, 45, 47, 55
  lip muscle, 25–33, 113
  lower jaw muscle, 35–41, 43, 113
  muscle, 3–8, 54, 74, 104, 110, 113, 118
  nose muscle, 17–24, 33, 113, 117
  reading, xi, xii, 40, 53, 54, 64, 65, 67, 122
    in whisper, 66, 67
    with questions, 14–16, 20, 24, 25, 29, 33, 40, 51, 53, 54, 63–66, 115, 116
  soft palate muscle, 55–66, 113, 121
  spilling, 42, 43, 45, 47
  tongue muscle, 41–55, 113
  waist muscle, 67–74, 113
  whispering, 65, 66
  yawning, 59, 60, 63, 66, 67

F

Facial expression, 9, 22, 23, 24, 25
Facial muscles, 5, 9, 114, 118
  collapsed, 11, 13, 117
  upper, 10
Fatigue, vocal, 3, 4
Floating up, voice, 11, 14–17, 20, 23–25,

128